Competitive Intelligence

Also by Chris West

Market Research

Competitive Intelligence

Chris West

palgrave

First published 2001 by
PALGRAVE
Houndmills, Basingstoke, Hampshire RG21 6XS and
175 Fifth Avenue, New York, N.Y. 10010
Companies and representatives throughout the world

PALGRAVE is the new global academic imprint of
St. Martin's Press LLC Scholarly and Reference Division and
Palgrave Publishers Ltd (formerly Macmillan Press Ltd).

ISBN 0–333–78669–6

This book is printed on paper suitable for recycling and
made from fully managed and sustained forest sources.

A catalogue record for this book is available from the British Library.

Library of Congress Cataloging-in-Publication Data

West, Christopher, 1940–
Competitive intelligence / by Chris West.
    p. cm.
Includes bibliographical references and index.
ISBN 0–333–78669–6
1. Business intelligence. 2. Strategic planning. 3. Competition. I. Title.

HD38.7.W46 2001
658.4'7–dc21   2001032788

10   9   8   7   6   5   4   3   2   1
10   09   08   07   06   05   04   03   02   01

Copy-edited and typeset by Povey–Edmondson
Tavistock and Rochdale, England

Printed and bound in Great Britain by
Creative Print & Design (Wales), Ebbw Vale

For Kelly

Contents

Preface

Whenever there is more than a single source of a product or service, competition is an inevitable and natural consequence. Suppliers take as many steps as they can to insulate their activities from aggressive competition but they invariably have to engage in some form of battle with each other in order to obtain a share of customers' business. The only question is whether it is a minor skirmish or all-out war.

Although military analogies are common, competition is more conventionally described as 'gentlemanly', 'fierce' or 'cut-throat', depending on its intensity and the manner in which it is conducted. Over time there has been a tendency to gravitate away from the 'gentlemanly' towards the 'cut-throat'. This coincides with a progressive transfer of power from suppliers to customers.

The last few decades of the twentieth century have seen a marked reduction in suppliers' ability to control markets. Monopolies and near monopolies, common in the nineteenth century, have almost disappeared. The cosy world of cartels and other supplier agreements that limit competition and seek to maintain orderly price regimes has also been severely restricted. This has been achieved by government competition policies which seek to ensure that customers (that is, voters) get good service and value for money by virtue of the fact that a number of suppliers have to compete in order to win their business. In consumer markets the process has been accelerated by the impact of consumer and other pressure groups that have encouraged and facilitated more informed buying as well as stimulating manufacturers to be more competitive.

A further inducement to compete has arisen from the fact that it has become increasingly difficult for companies to shield their customer bases from competitors. Traditionally suppliers have used geographical, product, service or even emotional barriers to create niches in which they are sole or dominant suppliers. However, improved physical communications, reduced product differentiation, better information flows and more discerning buying have not only given suppliers the ability to seek out and exploit wider customer bases, they have also enhanced the ability of customers to break out of the niches into which they have been classified and broaden the supply options for themselves. E-commerce represents the ultimate in this process since it maximises information flows and creates markets that are unrestricted by distance, nationality or language.

In competitive markets the quality of the competitive strategy is now as important as customer strategies in determining company performance. All strategies require information and competitive strategies are no exception. As a result there is an existing and growing requirement for competitive intelligence.

Although there has always been an interest in the activities of competitors, competitive intelligence as it is now practised was formalised in the USA only in the 1970s and 1980s. A major step in the formalisation process was the formation of the Society of Competitive Intelligence Professionals, which created a forum within which a wholly ethical intelligence-gathering process could be developed. This was essential if the business was to break away from the inevitable, but unacceptable, association with industrial espionage. The transfer of techniques to Europe took place initially in the late 1980s and early 1990s but really gathered momentum between 1995 and 1999 when a series of public conferences promoted competitive intelligence to wider audiences.

As we stand, competitive intelligence is still in the formative stages of its evolution. The more obvious techniques have been codified and described but new developments are constantly being reported in the professional journals. The Internet has had a profound effect on competitive intelligence, just as it has in other areas of research, but I am sure that equally important innovations will be discovered and introduced in the coming years. The reason for thinking so is that the innovations work both ways. As intelligence gathering becomes more widespread so do the techniques for restricting the outflow of information from companies. Counter-intelligence may be growing even more rapidly than competitive intelligence, thereby creating a spiral in which each side of the equation needs to find methods of circumventing initiatives taken by the other.

The main reason for writing this book is that although interest in competitive intelligence is growing extremely rapidly in Europe, there are very few published works which consider the subject from a European perspective. Books written by American authors are certainly of generic interest; the principles of competitive strategy and competitive intelligence are the same on both sides of the Atlantic. Furthermore, some American works provide extremely useful guides to European information sources. There are, however, fundamental differences between competitive intelligence as it is currently practised in the USA and how it is likely to emerge in Europe. These revolve around the extent to which information from government sources is freely available, the rules of disclosure, data protection legislation, the attitudes of company executives towards intelligence gathering and the ease with which it is possible to make contact with information sources. In some instances intelligence gathering is easier in the USA and in others Europe is a more open source.

Many of the early practitioners of competitive intelligence in the USA and Europe were former employees of security and military intelligence services and the police. They brought with them wide experience in intelligence collection and analysis techniques but also gave the business a 'James Bond' spin which, whilst undeniably exciting, tended to suggest a relationship between competitive intelligence and espionage. Since then a large number of practitioners in Europe have entered the business through market research and other more conventional channels. These entrants have neither had, nor desired, any military training and have had to develop their craft without resorting to subterfuge, illegal access, phone tapping, raiding dustbins or theft. They have to rely on diligence, ingenuity and deduction, which require a completely different mind-set and significantly different set of skills. In 1998 I had the pleasure of listening to a presentation to competitive intelligence professionals by Philip Knightly, the respected investigative journalist responsible for some of the major stories carried by *The Sunday Times*. He commenced his presentation by stating that journalists obtain their information in three ways: they could be given it by those who wish to publicise a cause, they could buy it or they could steal it. Would that competitive intelligence was that easy.

Despite the unfortunate associations, many of the current texts describe competitive strategy and competitive intelligence in military terms. The military analogy can be helpful in getting the message across but there are too many activities and techniques that are entirely appropriate in warfare but are not acceptable in corporate competition and competitive intelligence. This is particularly true of the spy for whom the end will always justify the means. Spies steal intelligence and get medals for doing so; competitive intelligence professionals who are caught stealing information get locked up.

This book will take a less dramatic line. Its primary focus is on the techniques for collecting and analysing competitive intelligence. Although I have not ignored the applications for the intelligence my stance is that of an information provider rather than a user. Many other books with the same title are happier delving into competitive strategy using descriptions of long-forgotten battles as analogies. They skim over intelligence gathering itself, which in my experience is by far the most difficult and mysterious part of the process.

The book has been written for the following readers:

- Competitive intelligence staff active within companies, particularly those confronted with the prospect of having to obtain competitive intelligence for the first time
- Competitive intelligence professionals working within CI consultancies
- Market research professionals
- Marketing staff seeking competitive intelligence
- Business strategists using competitor information

For those who are unfamiliar with competitive intelligence I hope that it will open their eyes to what can be achieved. For those who have had practical experience I hope it will open up some new methods by which research can be carried out.

The book is based on experience gained during a career in industrial market research and, latterly, competitive intelligence. Unlike our consumer research cousins, industrial market researchers include detailed examinations of competitors' activities in most of our projects, though in the early days the means by which we obtained the data were distinctly amateur. Aubrey Wilson, one of the first protagonists of industrial market research in the United Kingdom, tells how when conducting a survey on the woollen textile industry in the early 1960s he attempted to interview the owner of a mill in Scotland. This dour respondent insisted on taking down a hand-written note of every question that Aubrey proposed to ask before he would answer any of them. On reaching the final question he lifted his head, glared at the hapless interviewer from beneath shaggy eyebrows and shouted 'Get oot! Yer spying on me!' It has never been easy.

I first entered the specialist world of competitive intelligence in 1990 when Ruth Stanat of SIS International introduced me to the subject. I have always been grateful to her for what might have seemed at the time a minor piece of enlightenment. Since then I have worked on a wide range of projects in which it has commonly been essential to define the methods by which information could be obtained or deduced and then presented in an acceptable manner to clients. In many cases we undoubtedly had the dubious pleasure of 're-inventing the wheel', a process which I hope readers of this book will be able to avoid. It was nevertheless enjoyable and I am grateful to my former and current colleagues in Competitive Intelligence Services and to our many clients for the contribution they have made to the learning process.

Chipstead, Surrey **Chris West**

1 Competition

Competing is as natural as breathing and although the competitive process is not always enjoyable, winning is one of the most pleasurable human sensations. The desire to be a winner, to gain the prize or to succeed makes the effort or the pain of competing worthwhile. Competition pervades every aspect of personal, institutional and corporate activity. As individuals we spend our lives competing for success in school, in sport, for jobs, for partners and for recognition. Political parties compete for voters, government departments compete for funds, societies compete for members, charities compete for donations, tourist attractions compete for visitors and companies compete for customers. There are those for whom competition is a major reason for living; they are said to 'thrive on competition'. There are others who, in the interest of a quiet life, would prefer to get what they want without competing for it but, in the real world, they invariably find that it is impossible to avoid confrontation and competition completely. Companies would prefer not to compete, since doing so absorbs resources and reduces margins, but they recognise that competition is almost inevitable and, whether explicit or implicit, methods of dealing with competitors are an integral part of their business strategies.

The only way that companies can avoid competing completely is to be a monopoly but the opportunities to achieve this status are (now) extremely limited. Legislators and the economists that advise them have an unfortunate, though understandable, belief that monopolies are bad for customers. This is because historical evidence suggests that monopolists have a natural tendency to abuse their position by restricting supply below the level of demand and raising prices. In contrast, economists have defined 'free competition' as highly beneficial for customers, since it maximises supply and reduces prices to

1

the level at which it is just worthwhile for suppliers to remain in the business. Although Adam Smith was describing a world which was considerably less complex than that existing at the beginning of the twenty-first century, his summation of the difference between mono-poly and competition is timeless:

> A monopoly granted either to an individual or to a trading company has the same effect as a secret in trade or manufactures. The monopolists, by keeping the market under-stocked, by never fully supplying the effectual demand, sell their commodities above the natural price, and raise their emoluments, whether they consist in wages or profit, greatly above their natural rate.
>
> The price of monopoly is, upon every occasion, the highest that can be got. The natural price, or the price of free competition, on the contrary, is the lowest that can be taken, not upon every occasion indeed, but for any considerable time together. The one is upon every occasion the highest which can be squeezed out of the buyers, or which it is supposed, they will consent to give; the other is the lowest which the sellers can commonly afford to take, and at the same time continue their business.[1]

Although once common, it is hard to conceive that a true mono-poly would be sustainable in today's global economies. Apart from competition laws aimed at preventing companies gaining a position from which they can dominate markets, global communications and fast, low-cost transport has permitted larger numbers of suppliers to seek access to all markets. Where once local shops supplied vegetables grown in the neighbouring fields, today's supermarkets display vegetables from all parts of the globe and, apart from price variations, the notion of seasonal vegetables has all but disappeared. Various European state monopolies in telecommunications, postal services, transport, tobacco, drinks and minerals survived until the 1980s and 1990s but almost all of them died on the altars of privatisation and deregulation. Apart from the fact that governments no longer saw owning or running commercial enterprises as part of their mandate and had alternative uses for the funds that privatisation released, they had also realised that running businesses was not one of their strengths. One of the main arguments against monopolies – particu-larly state monopolies – was less to do with the fact that they charged high prices and more to do with the poor service they provided to their customers. Bureaucrats have always displayed a surprising insensitivity to the needs of those they are charged with administering, which, when transposed into a commercial environment, resulted in the antitheses of the customer care strategies that normal businesses were forced to embrace in the final quarter of the twentieth century.

By way of example, compare the prices for air travel on transatlantic routes with those that apply between major European cities. The cost of budget fares per transatlantic mile is in the order of 7 pence whereas between European destinations it can be fourteen times higher. There are a number of reasons why this is so but one of the most significant is the fact there is an abundant supply of seats on transatlantic routes whereas in Europe agreements between governments restrict seat supply. In other words, limited monopolistic practices are permitted in Europe, with a predictable effect on prices. Of course, the opposite of monopoly is not necessarily competition. In some markets a failure to control competition may result in a lack of supply because suppliers are unwilling to make the investments required to develop products or services which then fail to make an adequate return. The supply of pharmaceuticals, for which development costs are astronomic, is highly controlled for a period of time by patents and by the system of government approvals. This ensures that developers of new pharmaceutical products have sufficient time to recoup their development costs, and more, before they are exposed to the full force of competition.

Virtual Monopolies

The advantages of being a monopolist and the disadvantages of having to compete are sufficiently powerful to induce those that can to seek to create a quasi monopolistic situation for themselves. The main mechanism by which suppliers can avoid head-on conflict with competitors is a process well-known to marketers as product or service differentiation. This concept is closely related to the 'Unique Selling Proposition', first expounded by Rosser Reeves of Ted Bates as a key ingredient for successful advertising campaigns.[2]

Most suppliers accept that competition is inevitable but would prefer a situation in which it was unnecessary. Considerable research, design, development and creative resources are therefore devoted to efforts which will result in products or services which are clearly differentiated from those of competitors and may be perceived by customers to be unique – in other words, to create a form of monopoly. Unique products and services can result from or be complemented by a unique operational environment that clearly distinguishes the supplier from other companies active in the business.

Uniqueness can be real, in that a product has features or attributes not provided by competitive products, or it can be perceptual. The need to create perceived differences between products arises most strongly when real differences are difficult, if not impossible to develop and demonstrate. McDonald's does not have a monopoly of the hamburger market but it is widely perceived as a unique player within that market. This has happened because of its history as the first to develop a global burger business, its culture, its value proposition and its intensive promotional activity.

Differentiation can be sought in any aspect of a company's operations. Traditionally in the marketing process companies have sought to differentiate themselves from their competitors by:

- Production technologies
- Product features
- The raw materials used
- Price levels
- Discounts and rebates
- Distribution channels
- Delivery methods
- Delivery speed and reliability
- Promotional methods
- The perceptions they create for their brand
- Service offers
- Their location
- The company culture
- The staff they employ

Many of these are visible and therefore obvious to the competition; others are the invisible drivers of an end result, which is itself visible. For example, unique production technology or a unique source of raw materials can result in production cost advantages that translate into competitive prices.

However achieved, uniqueness is usually transitory in competitive markets. Unique product and service features can eventually be copied and even intangible advantages can be eroded over time by consistent promotion and publicity. The only long-term defence of unique positions is to innovate and create new forms of uniqueness.

Definition of Competition

A company's competitors are those organisations that can have an adverse effect on sales through their own success in winning business.

The most common definition of competitors is the narrow one of direct competition, which includes only those companies offering comparable products and services into the same target markets. In these situations the competition is head on and customers make a choice between suppliers that are all perceived as being capable of meeting their requirements in broadly similar ways.

However, competition also exists indirectly between suppliers that offer alternative and sometimes very different solutions to the same problem. In the traditional telecommunications market (often referred to as POTS – Plain Old Telephone Service) BT, AT&T, France Telecom, Deutsche Telecom and their other national equivalents were once monopoly suppliers. After privatisation, deregulation and the break-up of the monopolies competitors from very different backgrounds (cable TV and the utilities) emerged as direct competitors, as well as a host of new specialist telecommunications companies. Names such as Sprint, MCI, NTL, Telewest and Energis and a host of smaller companies offering low cost calls via calling cards or access numbers carved niches for themselves in the market, but the service was essentially the same.

However, the analysis of the competitive situation would be seriously flawed if it considered only the fixed line operators. The mobile communications market now accounts for a significant proportion of the total communications business and is competed for by a different set of suppliers in addition to the traditional carriers. The analysis would be further flawed if it excluded e-mail and text messaging, both of which are displacing voice communications, and, looking forward, effective voice communications over the Internet could cause a significant reduction in long-distance connections. The broadband technology that services the voice and data communications market also enables the transmission of pictures. This permits telephone companies to compete with terrestrial television transmissions and even the airline business, if video conference calling ever succeeded in reducing the amount of business travel.

Where Do Companies Compete?

There is a widespread and wholly understandable impression that the primary form of competition is that which takes place between companies *for customers*, in other words, that the main competitive battlefield is the marketplace. However, in the context of competitive intelligence it is important to recognise that this is very far from the case. Companies compete across the full spectrum of their activities and whilst the marketplace is extremely important, it is by no means the only competitive arena. Some of the key areas in which competitive action can have a profound effect on a company's performance are:

- Strategic – competition for acquisitions
- Technology – competition for patentable products and processes or for licences
- People – competition for the best staff
- Finance – competition for investors and funds
- Locations – competition for manufacturing, warehousing and office sites
- Suppliers – competition for raw materials or components
- Distribution – competition for shelf space
- Markets – competition for customers

In all these areas competition is significant only when there is an actual or impending shortage of whatever resource companies are seeking. In the battle for acquisitions the shortage is acute because at any one time there is normally only a few companies available to be acquired and a number of potential suitors. Competition for financial resources is rarely significant since the supply of funds that are available for good investments is not constrained to the point that companies need to fight for a share. In times of full employment competition for people can be acute, but at the bottom of the economic cycle supply can far outstrip demand. Similarly the supply of raw materials can oscillate from abundance to shortages.

Even in markets shortages of customers are not necessarily the case. There is rarely a shortage of demand for a real bargain. In such situations customers will soak up whatever supply is available, if only to stockpile. Demand is driven by a host of factors that include price and performance but also customers' anticipation of the future supply situation. Threatened shortages of essential products, such as food or petrol, will result in buying sprees that quickly deplete stocks. In such situations competition is irrelevant; customers will buy from whomever at whatever price they care to charge.

Marketing and Competitive Strategies

The principles of marketing were developed and codified in the postwar period when demand was growing rapidly and competitive pressure was relatively low. In many markets manufacturers could sell all they could produce and although they risked being left behind as superior products were developed, competition was not at the top of their list of worries. Marketing focused entirely on customers and was defined as a process for winning by offering products that met customer needs at prices they were prepared to pay. In his seminal work, *Innovation in Marketing*, written in 1962, Theodore Levitt barely mentions competition.[3] He concentrated on what was then deemed to be important, namely, customer retention, the evolution of markets and product development. Although outfoxing the competition was an inevitable part of this process, the emphasis was on the product and service stratagems that would be deployed, rather than direct competitive action. In a key chapter entitled 'Management Myopia',[4] Levitt attributes low growth to a management failure to spot developments that would make current markets obsolete. Targeted competitive action was relevant only for suppliers that were seeking exceptional growth and therefore needed to make gains in market share. The sequential recessions of the early 1970s, 1980s and 1990s resulted in an slowdown in overall economic growth and an overall trading climate in which even modest rates of growth required an increase in market share, unless companies were operating in specific high-growth niches.

At the same time the pressure on companies to compete more strongly has intensified.

This is a result of a number of clearly defined forces, which include:

- *Higher financial performance demands* placed on suppliers. Increasing financial demands of owners and shareholders have resulted in an injection of the killer instinct. The management of companies are required to meet ever more ambitious targets and certainly cannot afford to fail. They therefore defend their existing positions in their markets vigorously and are also driven to seek expansion
- *Diversification.* The need to protect and enhance the future growth of the business will often be interpreted as a need to diversify into new markets. If the markets they target are themselves new, competition may not intensify, as may also happen if the diversification is made by the acquisition of an existing participant. However, if a company enters an existing business as a new player then competition is automatically intensified
- *Globalisation* or geographical diversification. By reaching out into new countries global players intensify the competitive environment
- *Technology.* Developments in technology, and particularly the convergence of technologies, are enabling companies to challenge

incumbents in new markets and radically alter the competitive
environment
- *Outsourcing*. The trend towards outsourcing of key processes to
  those organised to carry them out more effectively and at lower
  cost can improve competitiveness by permitting companies to focus
  on the operations that they do best. The growth of 'virtual
  companies', which outsource all functions other than product
  design and overall management, is the ultimate expression of the
  outsourcing process. Providing the supplier of outsourced services
  performs well, outsourcing reduces the number of functions that
  companies need to control and manage and therefore the scope to
  create problems for themselves. By eliminating the need for
  investment in fully serviced companies, outsourcing reduces the
  cost of entry into markets and therefore encourages the formation
  of new competitors
- *Improved information flow*. The economist's definition of perfect
  competition includes the requirement for customers to have perfect
  knowledge of the products that are available and the prices for
  which they can be acquired. In the real world perfect knowledge
  rarely exists or is confined to small geographical areas (such as a
  street market). Suppliers have therefore been able to operate in
  markets that have been partially protected by ignorance. Long-
  term improvements in communications have gradually eroded such
  protection but the advent of the Internet has created a forum in
  which perfect information on product availability on a global scale
  is a real prospect

As a result of these changes, defending an existing market position
from attack or growing market share became serious marketing
objectives and share gains are difficult to achieve without engaging
in an outright battle with competitors.

Marketing has therefore evolved to embrace two separate streams
of strategy:

- The customer facing strategy, which is concerned with satisfying
  the needs of customers
- The competitor strategy, which is designed to win customers but by
  ensuring that the company and its products and services beat,
  outmanoeuvre or outflank the opposition

For maximum effect, customer and competitive strategies work
hand in hand, complementing each other in the common objective of
winning business. However excellent, a competitive strategy will not
compensate for serious deficiencies in a customer strategy for any

length of time, though it may provide breathing space whilst defects in the product or service offer are rectified. Similarly, however superb, customer strategies will eventually be unravelled and undermined by competitors.

The Competitive Environment

Writing in the 1980s,[5] Bruce Henderson described two extremes of competitive activity, *natural competition* and *strategic competition*. He described natural competition as an evolutionary process in which competitive activity progressed incrementally by trial and error. In a natural competitive state competitors adapt slowly to each other and to changes in the market environments in which they are operating. In contrast, strategic competition is revolutionary and 'seeks to make a very large change in competitive relationships'. Strategic competition can be initiated by suppliers who, for whatever reason, feel they can gain market share by engaging in an extreme bout of competitive activity. It increases the normal level of business risk and tends to be short-lived. However, a successful period of strategic competition will tend to encourage the perpetrator to repeat the exercise. If a competitor initiates a programme of strategic competition, retaliation is essential for survival. Those that are attacked will be required to defend their market positions or lose share. A successful defence may severely disadvantage the attacker and discourage further incursions.

Bouts of strategic competition are evident in many industries but particularly in retailing. In 1999 the major British supermarket chains, which had coexisted more or less peacefully for some years, were struck by a series of events that initiated a burst of strategic competition. Asda, the up-and-coming contender in the market, was acquired by Walmart, a major discount retailer in the USA. This more or less coincided with a period in which:

- Tesco, the market leader, had been gently flexing its muscles
- The British media were making increasingly loud protests about the differences between British and foreign prices for food and other consumer goods
- Three other rivals, Sainsbury's, Safeway and Marks & Spencer, had all been experiencing problems stemming from a failure to keep pace with developments in the marketplace

Asda and Tesco immediately embarked on a price war, which was heavily promoted as being in the consumers' interest. The weakened competitors were forced to follow suit or lose part of their constituency, the last thing they needed when trying to regroup and reorganise.

Mechanisms By Which Companies Compete

Competitive strategy is often likened to warfare. Marketing warfare has been written about extensively and most of the analogies are perfectly valid at a strategic level. However, there is one major difference between armed struggle and competing for customers, which means that the nature of the battle is radically different. In warfare the opposing forces fight over terrain. The primary measure of success is territorial gain and the subsequent domination or subjugation of those who live on it. In business competition is for customers and resources; they are, in effect, the terrain that is fought over. Unlike the landscape, customers and resources are active participants in the competitive process. It is their choices that determine the outcome of the battle. The landscape cannot reject its conquerors but customers can certainly refuse to be won, distributors can refuse to allocate enough shelf space and staff can refuse to be recruited. Force is not an option to overcome such resistance and must be replaced by persuasion which is effective only when it maximises the attractiveness of the offer, uses appropriate communication channels and maximises the financial benefit to the target. In a market environment this would be called marketing – persuading the target to do what you want them to do (that is, buy from you) by meeting their requirements more effectively than anyone else.

Scale

The perception of competition tends to vary according to the seniority and role of the staff member considering it. The perception stretches from a highly strategic view to short-term tactical issues. To the chief executive competition is defined as organisations and processes that can threaten the future viability of the company. At the level of the sales representative the competition that matters is any company or action that threatens a sale. At the intermediate level of departmental heads, interest in competition spans the short and medium term. Although concerned with losses of sales due to competitive action they are also concerned with performance in the budget period for which they are responsible.

Strategic competitive objectives

Clearly a competitive strategy is an integral part of any marketing strategy which needs to be shaped to take account of what competitors are doing. Where competitors exist the key role of the competitive strategy is to:

- Undermine competitors' offers so that the attractiveness of the suppliers' own offer is maximised
- Position the company so that any head-on conflict with competitors likely to drive down prices and margins is avoided
- Avoid activities in which the most likely outcome is a blood bath
- Anticipate competitors' actions so that their effectiveness can be neutralised

Tactical competition

Competitive intelligence has just as big a role to play in tactical situations as it does in the formulation of strategy. Indeed, many companies will recognise the tactical advantages that can be gained from intelligence more readily than any strategic benefits. Tactical activities are short-term responses to day-to-day situations that arise. They are 'cut and thrust' rather than broad sweeping developments.

Tactical competition revolves around the need to respond:

- When competitors implement unanticipated changes in their activities – this can include product launches, withdrawal from the business, changes in selling activity, new promotional programmes, changes in personnel
- When a change incurs within the customer base or in the supply chain
- When economic conditions change

Notes

1. Adam Smith, *The Wealth of Nations* (1776) Chapter VII.
2. Rosser Reeves, *Reality in Advertising* (New York, Alfred A. Knopf, 1961).
3. Theodore Levitt, *Innovation in Marketing* (New York, McGraw-Hill, 1962).
4. Originally published, and better known, as 'Marketing Myopia', *Harvard Business Review*, July–August 1960.
5. The Boston Consulting Group, *Perspectives on Strategy* (New York, John Wiley, 1998).

2 Intelligence

Competitive intelligence is the process by which companies inform themselves about every aspect of their rivals' activities and performance. It is an essential ingredient when planning not only marketing campaigns but also production programmes, human resources, finance and all other corporate activities that competitors can influence directly or indirectly. No battle can be fought without intelligence on the opposing forces. Just as card games are easier to win when players have either seen or deduced their opponents' hands and exams are easier to pass when the questions are known or guessed in advance, competition is easier to engage in when the current and future activities of the competitors are known or anticipated. In all competitive situations the accuracy and timeliness of the intelligence that is held may have a determining influence on the outcome of the engagement.

In battle where lives are at stake it is essential to know the terrain over which the battle will be fought, who the enemy are, their mentality and the resources at their disposition. It is preferable to know their intentions and it is extremely useful to know how they intend to achieve them and when and where they are likely to launch an attack. In fact the more information military commanders have at their disposal the greater their chance of winning. No student of military history can be in any doubt about the value of military intelligence and the major efforts that have been made to obtain it. The same level of criticality cannot be applied to a game of cards or even success in examinations, but in business, where the financial penalties for losing can be severe, the case for acquiring competitive intelligence can be indisputable.

The Applications for Intelligence

Intelligence on the marketplace within which competitive battles are fought, commonly called market or business intelligence, provides the essential background to all strategic and tactical decisions. It indicates the likely severity of the battle and the length of time over which it is likely to take place. It also indicates the marketing and promotional tools that competitors can use successfully to fight their battles and the messages to customers that are likely to produce the most positive outcome. But, more important than any of these, it provides a forward view of technology, customers and customer requirements that forewarns of significant change, thereby providing a basis for a strategy that differentiates companies from their competitors and permits some radical outflanking manoeuvres. The relationship between business or market intelligence and market research is extremely close. Only those who define market research narrowly as being concerned exclusively with customer surveys and focus groups will fail to see the connection.

Intelligence on competitors is used in three situations:

- Curiosity
- Emulation
- Anticipation

The most common, and least useful, is to satisfy an inevitable curiosity about other companies active in the same business. The level of curiosity may be tempered by an arrogant belief that competitors are irrelevant and is rarely deemed to be worth satisfying at a price. Curiosity is usually satisfied by information that is gathered through trade gossip, from staff that have previously worked in competitive companies, from published media and from informal contacts. No attempts are made to verify the information collected and such companies often live in a false competitive environment fed by inaccurate impressions and rumours in which it is impossible to defend themselves from surprise attack or even launch credible offensives.

Emulation is a more worthy application for competitive intelligence. It recognises that all companies have something to learn from their competitors – even if it is only that they have nothing to learn. The learning process can cover the full gamut of competitors' operations and its usefulness is recognised most readily:

- When a company has encountered a problem that it is having difficulty resolving with its own resources (so how do the competitors do it?)
- When existing or new competitors have launched an initiative that appears to be successful
- When competitors appear to be using superior technologies, achieving higher levels of productivity or performing better financially

Companies that use competitive intelligence only as a source of inspiration tend to be followers rather than leaders, content with the fact that they will be second to market with innovations and lagging in the performance race, but they are nevertheless benefiting from the knowledge gained by their competitors and leveraging their own skills and resources.

The most advanced application for competitive intelligence is that which enables companies to recognise current and future competitive threats and to devise stratagems that will neutralise their effectiveness and gain some form of competitive advantage. Advanced users of competitive intelligence tend to be:

- Companies that are active in businesses in which the competitive landscape is evolving rapidly and subject to major change
- Companies active in businesses that require heavy investments and long-term development programmes in order to remain credible players
- Aggressive players seeking rapid gains in market share
- Dominant players with major positions to defend
- Players that have recognised that they are seriously vulnerable to attack

Not surprisingly, the major users of competitive intelligence tend to be in information technology, healthcare (especially pharmaceuticals), financial services and e-commerce.

Companies to Watch

When determining the competitors that need to be studied it is wise to adopt the broadest possible definition of competition. Although the current threats may be obvious it is essential to consider potential future threats, and these can arise from well outside the current boundaries that delimit the business. As already described, competition is conventionally defined as comprising direct and indirect competitors. It can also be defined as current competition and potential future competition. The most worrying group in any market are the potential future competitors: those companies that have no current connection with the business, have not declared their hand but can have a devastating effect if ever they decide to enter.[1] Figure 1 illustrates the competitive structure that can exist in any market.

Most competitive intelligence is aimed at direct competitors – companies that sell identical products or services at similar prices to an identical customer base. These are the companies that are faced head to head in the marketplace on a daily basis and constitute the most immediate threat. Direct competitors are usually well-known. Only in new, rapidly evolving or highly fragmented businesses is it likely that companies are competing against suppliers of whose existence they are unaware and even then the competitive process usually ensures that their presence becomes known relatively quickly.

Indirect competitors are those that sell products or services that are not identical but compete for the same category of customers' expenditure. In the personal transport market cars in the same price and performance categories are in direct competition whereas manufacturers of motorcycles and providers of public transport services are indirect competitors. Indirect competitors need to be watched not

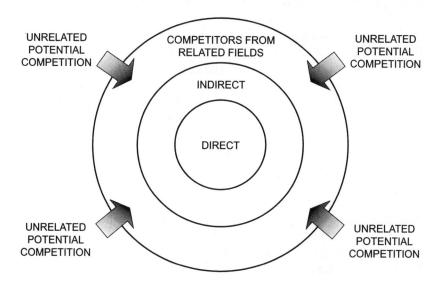

Figure 1 *Competitors to watch*

only because of the effect they can have on a market but also because they may broaden their product range and compete directly.

Outside the ring of direct and indirect competitors lies a further group of companies that are active in related businesses and have the skills and resources to diversify if conditions suggest that it would be profitable for them to do so. When diversifying such companies seek to maximise the use of the assets they have developed in their core or original businesses and in doing so may alter competitive conditions in the new markets. The emergence of garage forecourts as 24/7 grocery retailers is due to the fact that they attract a continuous mobile customer base, have parking space available and are already bearing the cost of long opening hours for their primary business. The entry of the supermarkets into financial services markets creates additional income earning opportunities from their customer base, uses the equity they have built in their brands and places them one step closer to being one-stop shops.

Further out still lie companies that have no current connection with a market but could at some stage decide to enter it. Radical diversifications are extremely difficult to predict since they are normally founded on interpretations of a skill base that are invisible to the outside world. When Virgin was launched as a record retailer only a brave observer would have predicted that at some future date the company would enter the airline and then the railway businesses. Now, having observed the power of the Virgin brand and its ability to carry the company into diverse markets it would be very easy (though not necessarily accurate) to suggest that ferry companies and cruise lines should consider them potential competitors.

Although new entrants from radically different businesses are difficult to anticipate they are also becoming more common. This in itself provides more evidence on which to base predictions. The realignment of IBM from a company supplying hardware to one offering a mix of hardware and consultancy services means that it is less surprising that a company like Hewlett Packard should make a bid for the consulting arm of PricewaterhouseCoopers.

One group that is often overlooked as a potential competitor is the customers. Despite the trend to outsourcing there is always a risk that customers will decide to make components for themselves or establish service departments that cut out external suppliers. The risk is greatest when customers' satisfaction with external sources deteriorates to low levels because quality is inadequate, supply is inconsistent, service levels are poor or prices are too high. Items that are deemed to be strategically important are more at risk than others.[2]

Narrowing the Field

Adopting a broad definition of competition has one major disadvantage – it can throw up large numbers of companies to watch. Studying hundreds of companies is clearly impractical, at least on any regular basis, and there therefore needs to be some mechanism by which competitors are placed in priority order. Obviously the companies that it is imperative to observe are those that can do the most damage to sales and profits in the short term. Within the ranks of direct and indirect competitors this can usually be determined by reference to:

- Size – large competitors generally have the resources and the power to do more damage than small competitors
- Management – superior management teams with proven records of success require closer watching than those with a reputation for mediocrity
- Aggression – competitors that have a record of being aggressive in the marketplace are likely to be more dangerous regardless of whether they are successful or not. Periods of aggression initiated by one supplier can cause turmoil in the market, to which participants have to respond
- Technology – competitors that are using significantly better technology have the capability to disturb the competitive balance, particularly if it can be converted into a product, performance or price advantage
- Product – competitors with identical or similar products require closer monitoring since they can be used as substitutes more easily and their actions can have an immediate impact on performance
- Customer base – competitors that service the same accounts or similar types of customers are inherently more dangerous than those that operate in more remote segments of the market
- Geographical proximity – this can arise when raw materials are shared, when the market is concentrated in a particular region or when one company is a breakaway from another. Competitors operating out of nearby locations are often close in many other senses; a high proportion of staff may have worked (or are being tempted to work) for the competitors and other resources may be shared, thus blurring distinctiveness in the minds of the customers
- Success – companies experiencing a run of success in the market need to be watched closely
- Profits – companies that are earning above-average profits may be establishing a resource base from which to broaden their competitive challenge

- Profile – high-profile suppliers, particularly those appearing frequently in the media, may be preparing the way for a major assault on the market
- Recruits – the recruitment of new management may also herald a change in pace in competitive activity

In the longer term it is necessary to consider the potential new entrants as well as those already active on the competitive scene. Since new competitors can emerge from many alternative sources and give few clues as to their intent, the problem of deciding which companies to watch is magnified many times. It can only be done effectively by carrying out a constant scan that seeks clues that suggest a possible interest in the market. The clues can be reasonably definitive or simply straws in the wind. The former will suggest that a company should be placed under close scrutiny; the latter that it should be examined from time to time to see whether more positive evidence is available. The clues that may be picked up in a scan are likely to include:

- Management statements that suggest that a diversification into a new market is being considered either for growth or as a replacement for poor earnings in current businesses
- The recruitment of new management known to have an interest in the market
- The development of a new technology that would facilitate entry into the market
- The establishment of partnerships that suggest a growing interest in new businesses and a mechanism for making an effective entry
- The purchase of a licence that could be used to enter the business
- Patented product developments

Alternative Applications for Intelligence-Gathering Techniques

The term 'competitive intelligence' implies that the techniques are valid exclusively for examining competitors and the competitive environment. Although the competitive intelligence community has indeed built its business around the analysis of competitors, the techniques are equally valid for other purposes. These include the analysis of companies that are being considered or targeted as:

- Acquisition candidates (which may also be competitors)
- Investment prospects

- Joint venture partners
- Suppliers
- Distributors
- Customers

Acquisition candidates

The acquisition process includes volumes of due diligence which normally concentrates heavily on the financial performance and prospects of the target company. The market and competitive environment are not usually ignored but it is rare for them to get more than a cursory examination by the teams of bankers, accountants and lawyers that comprise the typical acquisition team. Competitive intelligence techniques, which study the company covertly, can inject valuable insight into acquisition decisions on those aspects of the company that are unlikely to be revealed either by the figures or often the target company itself.

The main inputs are analyses of:

- The identity of current and potential competitors to the acquisition target
- The competitive positioning of the company within the markets it services
- Its strengths and weaknesses relative to significant competitors
- The types and levels of competitive pressures it is facing
- The sustainability of its market share and its ability to grow sales

A more refined use of competitive intelligence in an acquisition situation is to obtain insight into the internal structures, resources and cultures with a view to determining the degree of fit with the acquiring company. Cisco Systems, a voracious acquirer that made 70 acquisitions between 1994 and 2000, uses its competitive intelligence resources as an integral part of its acquisition team. A high proportion of Cisco's acquisitions are young companies just out of the early rounds of financing. With such companies it is essential to hold on to the key staff and for this to happen the company has to fit with the Cisco culture. Advance study of acquisition candidates considers their cultures and their leadership style and practices. This is used to identify those that stand a reasonable chance of being integrated without heavy staff losses. The success of this process can be measured by the fact that Cisco retains 70 per cent of the CEOs that it acquires.[3]

Investment prospects

Investments in companies by venture capitalists or trade investors are invariably preceded by a programme of due diligence to test the assumptions being put forward by the prospect. Data supplied by the company itself should rightly be treated with caution and verified independently. Whilst this is commonly accepted for the assumptions supplied about the market environment in which the company is operating it is rare to test the statements that the company makes about its organisation, internal workings and strengths. Competitive intelligence can be used to bridge this gap.

Joint venture partners, suppliers and distributors

The performance track record of all companies with which a potential relationship is being considered should be tested, particularly if the relationship is critical to future performance. It is essential to know whether a business partner is capable of living up to the promises they make, and researching their true capabilities and their reputation with other partners is more accurate than taking trade references and less expensive than finding out by trial and error.

Many of the so-called joint ventures between companies in the former east European countries and western partners were predicated on the assumption that the western partners would supply the financial resources that the eastern companies could use to expand their businesses. In a high proportion of cases the eastern companies lacked the management skills to use the finance with which they were provided and it soon became clear that without a major injection of management skills as well as finance, the joint ventures would fail. What was thought at its inception to be a joint venture soon became a full acquisition, which was not what the negotiators of the deals expected.

Customers

When pitching to business customers an in-depth and independent assessment of their activities, needs and satisfaction with current sources of supply can provide a basis for a winning bid. Suppliers that show an awareness of their customers' requirements are generally viewed more favourably than those that are ignorant and a bid that touches on real problems encountered by the customer in the past will add spice to the offer. It is even more helpful to know that specific accounts are dissatisfied with their current sources of supply and are open to competitive offers.

Alternative Routes to Intelligence

Any company seeking competitive intelligence has a number of alternative sources to turn to. In addition to those professionals that specialise in competitive intelligence using the techniques described in this book, they can consider:

- Companies that offer intelligence databases
- Market research companies
- Private detectives
- Companies that specialise in the investigation of corporate fraud
- Companies and individuals that carry out industrial espionage

Intelligence databases

Companies that have built databases of news and information on companies and markets have been quick to spot their usefulness for competitive intelligence and have repackaged their services accordingly. There is no doubt that a good database and clever search facilities are a major asset to analysts since they can save considerable time, speed up the search process and probably increase the amount of intelligence that is obtained.

Market research

The market research route to competitive intelligence has been in existence for many years. It has been part of the standard offer of research agencies that study industrial markets since the 1960s and the agencies that study consumer markets also have a long track record in providing basic sales and market share data for competitors. The use of market research for competitive intelligence is discussed further in Chapter 9 but it has to be appreciated that research agencies work on the fringes of competitive intelligence and not within its mainstream.

Private detectives

Private detectives are also on stronger ground for certain types of information. Their origins are usually in the police or military intelligence and their culture is one in which the end justifies the means. Whilst they will not engage in activities that are illegal they will have a different interpretation of where the ethical boundary line lies.

Corporate fraud

Companies that investigate corporate fraud are close in approach to private detective agencies, largely because they employ the same types of investigators. The clients they act for are under threat from activities that are illegal and it is judged fair to fight fire with fire. Although such companies study competitors, they are not a part of the competitive intelligence community as defined for this book.

Industrial espionage

Even though no real link exists between the methods by which competitive intelligence is gathered and those used in industrial espionage, there is a perceived link between the two activities. This is despite the fact that competitive intelligence is a natural and legal component of the competitive process whereas most of the techniques used for industrial espionage are completely illegal. Much is in the eye of the beholder. There are those that regard any attempt to collect information on their activities as a gross invasion of their privacy and will go to extreme lengths to stop it. In this they are aided by a press that much prefers stories about spies to anything as mundane and conventional as competitive intelligence. Press stories all too frequently elevate the most innocuous intelligence-gathering exercise to the equivalent of a spy ring organised by the former Stasi. Unfortunately the broader community that often aligns itself with the provision of competitive intelligence sometimes gives them cause to do so.

The temptation to initiate a programme of industrial espionage is strong amongst those with low ethical standards or whose need is so great that they are prepared to ignore their usual scruples. Competitive intelligence stands a reasonable chance of obtaining the data that are required but in many cases those that practise industrial espionage can almost guarantee that they will be able to obtain what is required. Where competitive intelligence will yield reasonable deductions on competitors' plans, the industrial spy will offer copies of documents and recordings of company meetings.

Notes

1. See D. Frances, K. Sawka and J. Herring, 'Competitors – Who to Watch, What to Watch, Who to Ignore and How to Tell the Difference', *Competitive Intelligence Review*, vol. 7, Supplement 1, 1996, pp. 95–100.
2. Deborah Sawyer, 'Defining Your Competition: Competition from Within: When the DIY Bug Bites Your Customers', *Competitive Intelligence Review*, vol. 7, no. 4, 1996, pp. 79–80.
3. Ammar Hanafi, 'CI at Cisco Systems: An Acquisitions Success Story', *Competitive Intelligence Magazine*, vol. 4, no. 1, Jan.–Feb. 2001.

3 The Development of Competitive Intelligence[1]

Market research has traditionally focused on the analysis of customers. This has never been to the exclusion of all other participants in markets, but 'customer focus' has been *the* distinguishing characteristic of an organisation that has embraced the marketing concept. The customer is the ultimate target of all marketing activity and understanding the customers' activities, requirements and expectations is, and will remain, an essential ingredient for the development of marketing strategies. However, customer analysis has never been able to provide answers to all marketing questions and other participants in markets have been studied and analysed regularly. These include distributors, specifiers, advisers and competitors. Each of them is a valuable source of intelligence for those attempting to define a winning strategy, though, to date, customer analysis has taken the lion's share of research budgets.

In many markets an unexpected consequence of widespread and total dedication to satisfying the needs of customers has been an intensification of the competitive environment. Products and services succeed best when they are genuinely unique. Market research can increase the chances of being unique, but only if competitive suppliers abstain from examining customers' requirements. What has happened in practice is that most if not all suppliers have researched the customer base extensively and, surprise, surprise, they have all arrived at exactly the same conclusions – or at least solutions which are so similar that the customers can barely differentiate one product or service offer from the others. Suppliers of products that are identical in specification and performance to those offered by competitors (such as most commodities, cement, steel, petrol and base chemicals)

24

have had to find methods other than product features by which to differentiate their offers. Typically they have relied on image-building, superior service strategies, deals with distributors, competitive pricing and discounting to create a differentiated offer. However, image, service, distribution and pricing requirements can be studied just as easily as product needs or even copied, therefore neutralising any market advantage that has been gained. In the absence of any further information, reducing prices or raising discounts may seem to be the only workable methods of winning customers, but it is a road to financial ruin. The consequence of these developments has been that companies have been forced to consider methods of attacking the competition whilst at the same time perfecting their offer to customers.

The prominence of customer analysis is not exactly under threat but as soon as trends in the research business, in the broadest sense, are examined, it is clear that an increasing proportion of resources is being allocated to the study of competitors. In Europe the sums spent on competitor analysis are still relatively small but dependence on customer analysis is being diluted as an increasing number of companies appreciate that overdependence on customer-driven strategies is increasingly likely to give rise to problems.

Competitive intelligence is far from new. Information on competitors has always been a component of tactical and strategic marketing planning. For centuries before marketing was a gleam in a Harvard professor's eye, companies have at least watched their competition, if for no better reason that to learn and pick up useful ideas. What we are considering is the development of competitive intelligence as a formal activity. In this sense it is following the path previously taken by marketing, customer analysis, strategic planning and a host of other business disciplines that have been converted from intuitive processes carried out by general management into specialist functions carried out by staff with formal training.

The Development of Competitive Intelligence as a Formal Activity

Having access to information on competitors is not the same as a structured competitive intelligence programme. In order to predict the development of competitive intelligence in Europe it is therefore necessary to understand the forces that make companies take the analysis of their competitors so seriously that they engage in intelligence programmes initiated and run by staff members with formal responsibility for the collection, dissemination and use of competitive intelligence. Normally, this process is not one which occurs in a single step but takes place over a period of time during which there is a growing awareness of the need to have a competitive strategy that is every bit as important as the customer strategies that are already commonplace.

In terms of their use of competitive intelligence, companies seem to move through a series of stages as illustrated in Figure 2. The first is *competitor awareness*. This stage is entered soon after a company is formed or even before, when the start-up is being planned. Being competitor-aware means that the key competitors are known and that there is some knowledge – usually incomplete and certainly unverified – about their products, their prices, the clients they have succeeded in winning business from, the market sectors they service and the staff they employ.

The organisation that is competitor-aware rarely uses the data that it holds other than for occasional *ad hoc* tactical exercises, such as competitive pricing decisions, or as an input to a business plan that has to be submitted to an external organisation, such as a bank.

As companies grow they tend to become *competitor-sensitive* – both in terms of their awareness of the damage competitors can inflict on their business and the need to win orders by competing more effectively. Unfortunately, being competitor-sensitive does not always increase the demand for information on competitors. An alarming proportion of competitor-sensitive companies continue to rely exclusively on informal information flows through their sales forces, business contacts and scans of the trade press, rather than a structured intelligence programme. When they do step outside the informal information channels the prime motive is usually emulation.

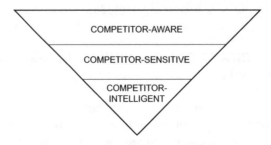

Figure 2   *The path to competitive intelligence*

They seek to copy what they perceive to be the best of their competitors' practices. There is nothing wrong with emulation as a business process, providing it is factually driven using techniques such as reverse engineering and competitor benchmarking, but it represents a very limited application for data that can be derived about competitors' activities.

The organisation which is *competitor-intelligent* is one that devotes serious resources to studying their competitors and anticipating their actions. This includes identifying competitors' physical and intangible resources, studying their organisations and their methods in as much detail as is practical and developing knowledge of their strategies and potential game plans. The competitor-intelligent organisation is set up to anticipate competitors' activities. It is continuously aware of the threats posed by competitors, the nature and seriousness of those threats and what needs to be done to counteract them. It recognises the need to look forward and predict the likely responses to actions it is proposing to take itself. It is also aware that the most serious threats may arise from companies that are not yet active in its business sector and may come from new entrants.

A summary of the conditions which apply in the three stages of competitive development is shown in Table 1.

There is a close parallel between the growth in competitor analysis, as described above, and the development of customer analysis. There was a time when organisations were only customer-aware. They knew

Table 1   *The three stages of competitive development*

Competitor	Data collection	Applications	Organisation	Systems for managing CI
Aware	Informal	Curiosity	None	None
Sensitive	Informal/ formal	Emulation	Marketing management information officer	Marketing information system
Intelligent	Formal	Anticipation	Competitive intelligence manager	Manual or computer-based CI systems

they had customers but took little account of customer requirements
in their product and service planning processes. Companies were
managed by staff with a technical or a commercial background, such
as engineers, chemists or accountants, and sold what they felt they
could produce best or most profitably. The sales representatives' task
was to dispose of the company's output at the best possible prices.
Progress was by a form of natural selection. The companies that grew
and survived were those that were lucky enough to develop products
for which there was a healthy demand. The rest fell by the wayside.
Those that survived were not guaranteed to continue surviving since
their products could always be superseded. Unless they kept pace with
developments in the market – often initiated by competitors – they
went under. Customer analysis was adopted when companies realised
that luck and natural selection were extremely poor ways of securing
the future of the business, especially when the tools were available to
make reliable predictions of customers' requirements from suppliers.

Factors Influencing the Growth of Competitive Intelligence

The progress from being competitor-aware to competitor-intelligent
is illustrated in Figure 3. It is driven by:

- The need to have a competitive strategy
- The ability to use the intelligence once it is gathered to contribute
  to the bottom line
- The ability to study competitors

Many organisations perceive a need but have no idea how to fulfil it.
Others may be aware that information can be collected but have no
idea how to develop a competitor strategy.

The need for a competitive strategy

The perceived need for a competitive strategy is determined by the
level or intensity of competition in the market serviced by the
company. If there are no competitors or if the competition is weak,
benign or inactive, there may be no point in wasting resources on a
competitive strategy. The industries that have been the quickest to
embrace competitive intelligence are those which experience the most
intense competition or where the competitive environment is changing

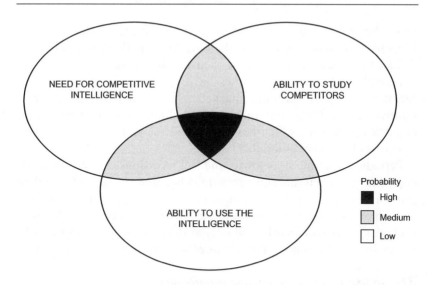

Figure 3   *Probability of competitive intelligence being used*

rapidly. In Europe, telecommunications, pharmaceuticals and financial services all fall into this category.

Around the world there have been a series of developments or events that have resulted in a major intensification of competition between suppliers. In summary these are:

- Privatisation
- Deregulation
- Liberalisation
- Global marketing
- Periods of economic recession

There are many industries that have led, and in some cases still lead, a life which has been heavily sheltered from the full blast of competition. The state monopolies and nationalised industries are the leading exponents of this happy condition. Telecommunications, electricity, gas, water, steel, the airlines, broadcasting and some of the automobile manufacturers have all been protected at some stage in many countries. Privatisation signalled the end of protection and has resulted in an intensification of competition, sometimes to an alarming extent.

Deregulation has similarly intensified competition. The accountancy and legal professions and the airline business have all become far more competitive when the regulation of those businesses ceased.

Once the gloves were taken off, even the most traditional organisations have become addicted to the bare-knuckle fighting required to defend their business or increase their market share.

Global marketing programmes have resulted in more companies seeking to supply national markets. These have often imported innovative products and marketing techniques from their home countries or regions which have disturbed the status quo in the new territories they have entered.

Periodic economic slowdowns and full recessions can also intensify competition. When markets grow quickly suppliers can achieve their growth ambitions without impinging on their competitors' territories, as long as they are not overambitious. When markets slow down or decline, growth can be achieved only at the expense of competitors by increasing market share. This requires a clear competitive strategy.

The ability to use competitive intelligence

There is generally a high awareness of the tactical applications of competitive intelligence. It requires neither training nor experience to work out that knowledge of competitors' prices, sales techniques, staffing policies, training programmes and terms and conditions of business would facilitate a winning sales pitch. What is less well developed is the strategic use of intelligence to position a company so that future competitive threats can be anticipated and countered. The skills to do this are still a rare commodity.

Interest in competitive strategy was kindled and nurtured by the publication of books such as Michael Porter's *Competitive Advantage* and *Competitive Strategy* in the 1980s.[2] This was accompanied by a short flirtation with marketing warfare which focused on beating the competition by adopting military tactics. Although marketing warfare was great fun it was rarely practical. Many of the analogies were stretched far too much to be really useful. Nevertheless, business school courses and external training programmes have led to greater awareness of the elements of competitive strategies and have heightened the need for intelligence on which they can be based. They are also increasing the supply of analysts that can use the data.

The ability to study competitors

The final driver of development is the ability to obtain a regular supply of accurate intelligence. As already stated, most companies have access to internal sources in the form of published reports, industry newsletters, company websites, the trade press and their own sales forces. Whilst these sources are capable of providing a foundation level of intelligence, they are rarely harnessed fully and, even then, are rarely adequate. A surprisingly high proportion of companies are unaware of the fact that primary data collection and analytical techniques exist to provide a full analysis of individual competitors and provide a tool for predicting competitor actions.

This situation is changing gradually as more professionals are allocated to the task of competitor analysis and budgets for the acquisition of intelligence are being established. In this respect European business lags behind the United States by several years where the competitive intelligence profession has already matured and has become an established part of the armoury of management techniques.

Factors Inhibiting the Growth of Competitive Intelligence

There are also some serious constraints on the growth of competitive intelligence. The most important of these are:

- Data protection legislation that has been enacted at national and European Community levels
- Fears that competitive intelligence is unethical
- Counter-intelligence
- Failure to deliver on promises

Very broadly, data protection legislation places severe restrictions on the amount of information that can be reported on *individuals*.[3] The collection and analysis of information on companies is not constrained, except to the extent that it involves an analysis of owners, directors or individual staff members. In many situations this is not a serious problem but the legislation has a much wider effect on competitive intelligence than the legal stipulations.

In addition to the actual constraints data protection legislation can reduce respondent willingness to cooperate because of the fear that they might be infringing the law. It can be used as a convenient excuse for those that do not wish to cooperate.

Fear of engaging in unethical activity is also a powerful constraint. Discussions on competitive intelligence very quickly turn to the subject of industrial espionage, which in the view of many people is the same thing. It can take a lot of explaining to convince marketing staff that it is possible to collect useful intelligence by wholly ethical techniques and that because it is useful it does not have to have been stolen. To the cynical, the code of conduct under which competitive intelligence is carried out suggests that it will rarely come up with anything useful. This is far from true but the case needs to be demonstrated convincingly.

Counter-intelligence measures, which seek to control the outflow of potentially sensitive information, are already installed in many companies. Their effect is to frustrate not only competitive intelligence exercises but also legitimate market research activities. Not surprisingly, as the profile of competitive intelligence rises so does interest in counter-intelligence. This may result in the cart arriving before the horse with counter-intelligence techniques in place before competitive intelligence becomes established as a substantial business.

The final threat to the development of competitive intelligence would be a failure to deliver on its promises. This could happen if competitive strategies do not result in the gains that are expected or if the data that are specified could not be obtained. There is a real danger of both, especially the latter. Much of the data that are being specified for competitive intelligence exercises is highly sensitive and there is always a significant chance that they cannot be obtained at a cost which is regarded as acceptable or even at all. There are, for example, cases of companies wishing to know who is bidding for particular contracts and what prices they have included in their bids. This is an unreasonable expectation but pointing this out can cause dissatisfaction with the process.

Notes

1. This chapter is based on a paper given by the author at an ESOMAR Conference *Marketing and Competitive Intelligence: Understanding the Impact*, Geneva, 1999.
2. M. Porter, *Competitive Advantage*, Macmillan, New York, 1985; M. Porter, *Competitive Strategy*, The Free Press, New York, 1980.
3. See Chapter 15.

4 Framework for Competitive Analysis

The intelligence needs of any organisation must be driven by the applications for which the intelligence is to be used. This applies across the board regardless of whether it is marketing intelligence, business intelligence or competitive intelligence that is being considered. The need for competitive intelligence derives directly from an organisation's competitive strategy and from a wide variety of tactical situations in which the organisation squares up to competition on a daily basis.

At a strategic level intelligence is used to define:

- How an organisation can be positioned (or repositioned) in order to win business from competitors
- The likely responses that competitors will make when challenged by a new market initiative
- Future changes in the shape and structure of the competitive environment that may enhance or detract from the organisation's ability to sell

Positioning against the competition requires a clear understanding of each competitor's own stance in the marketplace and their apparent objectives. All markets are made up of a mixture of:

- Competitors that seek to lead, in terms of technology, innovation, service and price, and others that are content to follow
- Competitors that seek to dominate in the market-share rankings and others that exploit favoured niches
- Competitors that are aggressive attackers and competitors who defend the territory they have already won
- Competitors that rely on their size and those that exploit the nimbleness that is a common consequence of being small

Within this environment the organisation must select a competitive strategy that it feels will enable it to meet its own corporate objectives. Depending on the characteristics of the competition it may also feel that the objectives themselves should be reshaped to ensure that they are realisable. An important ingredient in both activities is an assessment of the competitors' ability to sustain the positions they have chosen and their vulnerabilities to competitive attack.

Competitors' responses when under attack can be observed over time and are a function of their objectives and their resources. They also reflect the personality of the leadership and their interpretation of how best to wage competitive war. With a few notable exceptions business leaders tend not to have profiles which are as high as those of generals in battle but this does not mean that they are any less important in determining how a competitive action will be fought, only that by being less well-known they are less predictable.

No competitive environment is static. It changes its shape according to the activities of companies that are in the business, the emergence of new entrants and changes in the various marketplaces that the competitors service. The actions of companies in a market may be influenced strongly by what is happening in other markets in which they are operating. It is quite possible for a competitor to reduce its activity level purely because it is experiencing problems in another market.

Mapping the Competitive Landscape

Companies coming to competitive analysis for the first time generally require a map of the competitive landscape within which they are operating. Although the major direct competitors may be well-known, competitors that are active in specialist niches and on the peripheries of the business may be less clearly visible. Companies in start-up situations or entering new markets obviously have a greater need for maps of the competitive landscape than those that have been active in a business for many years. However, experience is sometimes a poor guide to competition, particularly if the business is evolving rapidly, and can be completely inadequate when looking forward to the structure of future competition. In all markets, new entrants from adjacent markets or from converging technologies represent a constant threat and create a requirement for regular updating of the competitive map.

When considering the competitive landscape, participants in a business are often poorly placed to recognise the full spectrum of competition they may be facing. Their view tends to be blinkered by the parameters of their own activities, which restricts their ability to recognise suppliers as competitors unless they are in a broadly comparable position to themselves. Those that are carrying out the mapping process must have a free hand to include not only direct competitors but also those that are indirectly competing for the same segment of the customers' budget. This may involve looking at competition through the eyes of the customers by asking questions that determine which suppliers customers consider as being capable of solving their problem. Even outside technology markets, where it is broadly accepted that there are many different ways of providing a solution, this process can yield surprises.

Most competitive situations are sufficiently complex to defy simplification and a map of the competitive landscape is the key to understanding the nature of the competitive battle to be fought. The map shows the number of organisations competing for customers and classifies them according to their size and the share of the market that they hold. It provides a basic profile from which a number of assumptions can be drawn about the competitive battle. Clearly a map that is this simple does not provide all of the answers but it represents a starting point, which can be elaborated as more intelligence becomes available.

The map, based on company size and market share, can be presented as a grid, which at its simplest would have four segments. In Figure 4 these have been described in terms that characterise the likely strategic posture of the companies that occupy each box.

Occupants of the competitive landscape

As defined above there are six typical occupants of the competitive landscape each with a different perspective and each representing a different type of threat to the other occupants.

Defenders

In slow- or low-growth markets, large companies with large market shares will often be in a defensive position. They have a lot to lose but also have the resources required to prevent loss by erecting barriers around their business and engaging in fierce defensive actions, if required. Obviously, the need to defend depends on whether they are

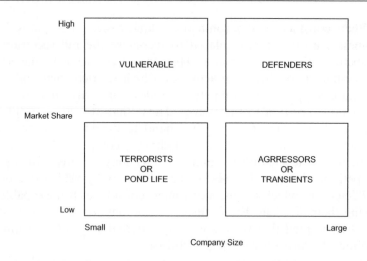

Figure 4　*The competitive landscape*

being attacked but they may engage in preemptive action in order to deter potential aggressors as well as brutal and punishing campaigns against those that threaten their positions.

Aggressors

The main aggressors in the competitive landscape sit in the large-company, low-market-share box. If the market is attractive enough they are likely to be considering how to expand their market share. The two options for them are organic development and acquisition. The juiciest targets for them to attack in any organic driven programmes are those companies in the defender box. They will also consider companies in the other two boxes as acquisition targets. Although each company holds only a small market share and will yield only a small volume of sales, their attraction is likely to lie in the staff, technology or expertise that has enabled them to penetrate the market.

Transients

Some of the companies in the large-size/small-share box will have a passing interest in the market and are likely to seek an orderly exit. If their small share is the result of an attempted market penetration that has failed to yield significant results or is a legacy business that is no longer regarded as core to the company's development, they will consider a disposal either to an existing participant or to the management.

Terrorists

The terrorists in the bottom left-hand box are small both in size and market share but have some unique or attractive component in their offer. It is this that has enabled them to gain access to the market and has provided them with a basis on which to shake up the status quo. Typically they are underpinned by some unique technology, a method of doing business or exceptional staff that they are exploiting as aggressively as their resources will permit. They cannot be written off as their activities may be underwritten by a venture capitalist or some other external source of capital. Their seriousness as competitors depends on the financial resources they command and their personal and corporate objectives. These will determine whether they are in business for the long term as independent units, whether they are seeking to build a position and then exit by selling to the highest bidder or whether they will hang on until their financial resources are depleted and are then forced to seek a buyer.

Pond life

Pond life describes small companies that have no unique product or service to offer and have captured market share because of contacts, proximity to customers or because they offer lower prices. In highly fragmented markets the pond life as a whole can account for a significant proportion of the market and apart from siphoning off business can also set price expectations amongst customers that disadvantage the activities of more significant suppliers.

The vulnerable

The companies that are vulnerable are those that are small but have captured a large market share. By definition they do not exist in large markets and do not coexist with defenders. However, they do emerge in new markets (such as the dot com businesses) which they have commonly been instrumental in creating. Their vulnerability arises from the fact they may lack the resources to defend the position they have established. They are prime acquisition targets because they offer larger companies an easy route into business.

Multiple landscapes

Most companies of any size operate in more than one landscape each of which can display significantly different competitive climates defined by the characteristics of each separate business. High-level landscapes, such as engineering, business services or banking, are virtually useless even to companies that are active in all segments of those businesses. It is essential to focus on the landscapes that describe specific segments of the business in which a company operates and within which separate competitive line-ups exist. Some competitors may be common to all landscapes but there will normally be a number of suppliers that are encountered uniquely in one landscape.

Drivers of Behaviour and Change

The key drivers of behaviour and change within the competitive landscape are a number of external forces and conditions within the companies that occupy the landscape. To understand the current situation and future trends fully, competitive intelligence provides insight into all aspects of competitors' operations but the data normally fit within the following topics:

- The competitive climate
- Cultivation

The competitive climate (market and business intelligence)

The simple description given above is rarely enough to explain the development of a competitive landscape. To do that it is necessary to study the competitive climate, which is itself a function of the general business environment. As in nature, the competitive climate is determined by a number of elemental forces that combine to create conditions that are periodically stable or highly changeable. The main forces that determine the climate in the competitive landscape are:

- Market size
- Market growth

- Market trends
- Profitability
- The existence of parallel landscapes

Market size

Large markets can have very different competitive climates to small markets. Large markets offer opportunities for companies of all sizes and because they also tend to be mature markets they have a structure and competitive climate that have evolved over a long period of time and settled down to some form of orderly coexistence between participants. Within large markets skirmishes can occur in particular corners without disturbing the overall equilibrium. In contrast small markets can be highly volatile. Large companies are not normally attracted to small markets and may avoid them unless they see them as interesting niche businesses or as offering high growth potential. Even then, they often find them difficult to exploit because their culture does not permit them to operate effectively when the pickings are small and they cannot use their size in order to gain advantage. Small markets therefore tend to be serviced by small or medium-sized companies.

Market growth

Growth is another conditioning factor. High rates of demand growth tend to lessen the level of competitive pressure by making it possible to achieve sales objectives without increasing market share. In high-growth markets the aggressors may be less aggressive and the defenders less interested in building their defences. However, high growth rates may also suck in significant amounts of pond life and also provide the terrorists with fertile ground on which to establish a business base from which they can assail the market in future.

Market trends and profitability

Market trends, such as changes in the structure of the business, improvements in technology, the emergence of new customer groups and fundamental changes in the way business is carried out, can have a significant effect on the competitive landscape. They can encourage new entrants or discourage traditional suppliers that cannot or do not wish to keep pace with the changes that are occurring. They can boost the profitability of companies positioned to take advantage of the trends and reduce the profits of those that are not. The emergence of e-business is a major example of a trend that will eventually change the patterns of activity in all segments of business. By providing suppliers with a direct route to their customer bases, e-business creates a clear threat to traditional intermediaries and provides opportunities for those that can embrace e-business techniques. Even if the dot com businesses themselves fail to succeed they will have shown traditional businesses how to revitalise their operations and change the basis on which they compete.

Parallel landscapes

Parallel landscapes are those that are close to the landscape being studied but sufficiently different to be regarded as separate. This importance lies in the fact that even if they are not populated with directly or indirectly competitive suppliers, they may contain companies that could be sufficiently attracted by the business to diversify into it. Credit card companies, such as American Express, have been diversifying to the extent that they are emerging as direct competitors to accountancy practices, who have themselves diversified so that they compete with merchant banks as sources of investment capital. Unless the parallel landscapes are identified and understood it is unlikely that the full extent of the competitive battle will be understood.

At times there can be a strong tendency for parallel landscapes to merge and obliterate the boundaries between businesses that existed previously, thereby causing dramatic change to the competitive situation. In the 1980s it would have been possible to define five separate competitive landscapes concerned with the delivery of mail and the shipment of products:

- Traditional post offices
- Courier companies
- Road transport companies
- Airfreight companies
- Warehouse operators

Competition was largely within each landscape, which was occupied by different suppliers. Since then companies active in all five landscapes have built up their service portfolio to such an extent that the landscapes have converged into a new format. Logistics has emerged as a service that encompasses all forms of storage, transport and distribution and offers a single link between suppliers and customers. The last bastion to fall is the post office who, in exchange for taking on a broader distribution role, are faced with the prospect of losing their monopoly in the delivery of letters.

Cultivation

Continuing the analogy further, landscapes can be cultivated by active human intervention as well as by natural forces. The cultivators in a competitive landscape are the companies that occupy it, each seeking to alter what existed before by the processes of re-shaping, re-planting and fertilising in order to achieve conditions that are more conducive to their own performance and less advantageous to their competitors. They do so by a variety of means including product innovation, creating new needs, introducing new routes to market, changing customer attitudes and perceptions and by pricing.

Cultivation can either be part of a deliberate competitive strategy aimed at increasing market share or a consequence of competitors' natural evolution. Although it is rare for any initiative to be taken without some consideration being given to the effect it is likely to have on competitive performance, activities that evolve naturally tend to be more predictable and less threatening than those which form part of a competitive assault. For this reason alone it is essential to differentiate between the two. This point can be covered by asking not only what competitors are doing but why they are doing it and in what part of the landscape they are active.

The most active cultivators are likely to be the 'terrorists', consistently seeking to improve their positions by innovative actions and with little to lose if they fail. Aggressors may also be drawn into using cultivation activities as a means of disturbing the status quo. Defenders and the vulnerable are better served if the landscape remains unaltered though they too may be drawn, albeit reluctantly, into cultivation if they are threatened. However they originate, cultivation activities by companies can be as effective as the competitive climate in changing the nature of the competitive landscape and therefore need to be given equal priority in the analysis programme.

Types of Intelligence

Financial intelligence

Most profiles include an assessment of the financial performance of subject companies. This can be relatively straightforward in the case of all public companies, subsidiaries and privately held companies in Europe that have to place copies of their reports and accounts with the relevant authorities. It is also feasible when a regulatory authority publishes key performance data for the companies active in the business it is regulating, as is commonly the case for utilities and telecommunications. However, it is far more difficult in the case of private companies in the USA, for divisions of companies or for specific locations.

One of the most challenging tasks for a competitive intelligence analyst is to construct a profit-and-loss account for a business unit for which no published financial data exist, relying exclusively on an analysis of sales and estimates of costs. Hard data on competitors' detailed cost structures are rarely obtained as they are rightly regarded as highly confidential. The peripheral data that might be expected to provide important clues to a cost structure can usually be interpreted in a number of different ways. Accountancy is far more of an art than a science and even the competitors themselves will employ different conventions when accounting for their performance, depending on what they are trying to prove. There are of course some facts that cannot be easily distorted and that are worth having. Legitimate targets can include the prices paid by competitors for their raw materials or their energy, wage levels, other (non-wage) costs of employment, manning levels, production efficiencies, selling and marketing costs and outsourcing costs, all of which can provide important insight into subsidiary or divisional profitability, but no amount of analysis will provide some of the key items, such as depreciation charges, that would permit the construction of an accurate P&L.

Technical intelligence

In manufacturing companies technical intelligence includes the study of competitors' products, technology, manufacturing processes, research and development and technical support, all of which make major contributions to the ability of a company to compete effectively now and in the future. In service businesses it is the basis of the service offer and the methods by which the service is to be delivered that need to be studied.

Sales and marketing intelligence

The study of a competitor's sales record including an analysis of segments serviced, customers won and lost, market share and sales volumes provides a clear indication of performance. An analysis of marketing resources, processes, procedures and routes to market, coupled with a measurement of the volume (and cost) of marketing activity, provides a highly visible barometer of where a company is directing its effort and the intensity with which it is pursuing its sales objectives. Analysis of the language used in advertisements and promotional literature can also indicate how the competitor sees itself and tells something of the culture that is prevailing within the organisation.

The study of marketing activities can be extended to cover the results of the process in terms of the customer base the company has succeeded in acquiring and its key accounts. The analysis can be taken further to consider the awareness of competitors, the relationship between competitors and their client bases, satisfaction with competitors' performance, the levels of client loyalty and the image of competitors in the marketplace.

Pricing and discount intelligence

Price is one of the key elements in the competitive battle and although competing on price is widely regarded as an admission of failure, it may nevertheless be the final arbiter of who wins the business. Prices are either extremely easy or extremely difficult to collect. Those that are displayed or published can be easily observed but where prices are tendered more sophisticated methods are required in order to obtain them. Discounts to retail and wholesale channels, for volume purchases or to encourage particular target customer groups may also be largely invisible but still a significant factor in the supplier selection process.

People intelligence

The methods by which companies compete, the intensity of competitive action and the use that is made of the range of physical and financial assets owned by companies is dependent entirely on people, especially key decision-makers such as owners, management and advisers. To understand competitors it is therefore imperative to know as much as possible about the history and motivations of the management that drive decisions and the calibre and experience of the staff that have to implement them. It is also necessary to know the pressures that are being placed on the company from external sources. Owners, be they individuals or parent companies, bankers, auditors, management consultants and partner companies can all exert pressure or provide advice that influences the objectives of competitors and the actions they take to achieve them.

Operational intelligence

Operational intelligence covers the way in which competitors are organised, staffing levels, staff efficiency, the ways in which the company makes decisions, partnerships and the prevailing culture within the company. Much of this intelligence can be used for benchmarking and providing an explanation for variances in financial performance.

Key Intelligence Topics

Most organisations have neither the physical resources nor the budget to study every aspect of their competitors' performance. Nor do they often have the need to study everything. One of the main tasks of the staff responsible for competitive intelligence is to ensure that only those questions that will make a contribution to the performance of their company are asked. There are many topics on which intelligence may be nice to have but far from essential. Given the cost of intelligence collection it is imperative that resources are concentrated on the essential rather than the peripheral.

Defining key intelligence topics is a process, not a task.[1] The most valuable topics are those that managers will actually use in their planning and marketing programmes and, although competitive intelligence staff can provide guidance to line managers on their requirements, they cannot make the final decisions. One of their most valuable contributions is to steer managers away from topics on which it will be impossible to provide meaningful intelligence, either because it could not be collected using legal methods or because whatever is collected will have so many caveats that it will be virtually impossible to use. Oddly enough there is also a need to educate managers on what it *is* possible to obtain. The intelligence sights are set too low even more frequently than they are set too high.

Initiating an intelligence programme is the most difficult part of the process since management and the competitive intelligence staff can be equally ignorant on what is required, what is likely to be used and what can make a contribution to performance. At this stage a checklist of topics that could potentially be covered is helpful as a starting point for decision-making (see Appendix – Competitive Intelligence Checklist). Once a range of topics have been identified the next task is priority setting, which involves categorising intelligence into that which is regarded as essential, that which is useful and that which should be obtained only if it proves possible within the constraints imposed on the competitive intelligence programme. As managers become regular users of intelligence and intelligence becomes embedded in their decision-making process the task of defining what is required becomes considerably easier. Regular meetings need to be held between intelligence collectors and intelligence users at which intelligence is discussed and evaluated. These normally identify the priority topics for future intelligence programmes and set them in priority order.

An active and effective competitive intelligence department sits at the centre of a network of internal and external contacts. It:

- Collects requirements from the various intelligence users within the company
- Eliminates the duplications
- Assigns the collection tasks to internal and external resources
- Assesses the results and calls for clarification and extension where needed
- Feeds results back to the users
- Meets with users to discuss the results and collect further needs.

Format for Collecting and Presenting Intelligence

There are three formats within which intelligence can be collected and presented for use:

- Profiles of competitors
- Tactical intelligence
- Tracking
- Strategic intelligence

The choice of format depends on the stage in the analytical process, the time and budget available and the applications for which the data are required.

Profiles of competitors

Competitor profiles are a core component of most competitive analysis. A profile can be comprehensive or relatively superficial, depending on the application for which it is intended. Full competitor profiles provide a holistic view of competitors by bringing together the intelligence topics discussed above.

The ultimate objective of a profile is not simply to describe the activities of competitors but to draw deductions about their future objectives, the means by which they intend to achieve them and the intensity with which they will pursue growth or defend an existing position. The analysis will commonly cover their commitment to the business, their intended growth rates, their future positioning and the market segments they are likely to be targeting. Direct intelligence on these subjects is rarely obtained using the methods available to competitive intelligence analysts but a full profile can support reasonably detailed deductions.

Tactical intelligence

A high proportion of competitive intelligence exercises are devoted to obtaining tactical intelligence. This covers a wide range of enquiries of varying levels of sophistication. Routine work involves the collection of:

- Company brochures
- Product samples
- Price lists
- Credit agreements

More demanding tactical intelligence exercises can provide information on any aspect of a competitor's operations such as:

- Orders gained
- Key customers
- Equipment purchases
- Sales force size and quality
- Product splits
- Terms and conditions
- Sources of raw materials
- Marketing and promotional activities
- Distribution channels
- Export markets

Factual intelligence is commonly required quickly to meet an immediate need and there is invariably only a short period of time to carry out the research.

Tracking

Competitors can be studied either on a one-off basis or by tracking their activities at regular intervals. In practice most companies monitor the activities of their competitors, at least on an informal basis, and the decision whether to elevate this to a formal tracking study depends on the amount of change which is occurring or is anticipated, and the intensity of competitive activity.

Tracking studies are particularly beneficial when competitive activity is in a state of rapid evolution. This can take the form of new entrants into a market or an increase in competitive aggression by established suppliers because they wish to launch new products, increase their market share, enter new segments of a market or defend their position against predators.

Changes in competitive activity can be triggered not only by the ambitions of the competitors themselves but also by external factors such as the introduction of new technologies and structural changes in the market. Both of these can create opportunities for significant realignments in the relationships between suppliers and the customer base.

In such situations one-off analyses are soon out of date. Tracking studies not only keep the information current but also permit a continuous realignment of the competitors that are covered and the intelligence that is sought.

The frequency at which the activities of competitors are re-examined in a tracking survey depends on the pace of change and the ability of the company to use the output. Monthly tracking surveys are common but to make them worthwhile there must be sufficient change each month to justify the cost and effort of collecting the data. It is also imperative that systems exist within the company to use the data on a continuous basis. There is little point in collecting information only for it to sit on a database.

The main problem with tracking surveys is contact fatigue. The process normally demands a network of contacts within and outside the target companies. Whilst these can be induced to cooperate for a while, there invariably comes a stage at which even the most unwary respondents begin to get suspicious. Occasional interest in a company can be given some plausible explanation; continuous interest is much more difficult to explain.

Strategic intelligence

Knowing who competitors are, what they are doing and what they are capable of doing has an immediate value but for most companies it is infinitely more useful to identify their competitors' strategies. Intelligence on strategic objectives and how competitors plan to achieve them provides valuable clues to competitors' reactions to situations as they arise. With strategic intelligence it is also possible to anticipate competitors' actions and provide an opportunity for pre-emptive action.

The Time Dimension

Time is a dimension that is critical to competitive analysis and defines, amongst other things, the difference between the intelligence that can be obtained and the intelligence that is required. As shown in Figure 5 the three time dimensions within which intelligence operates are (not surprisingly) the past, the present and the future. The past is

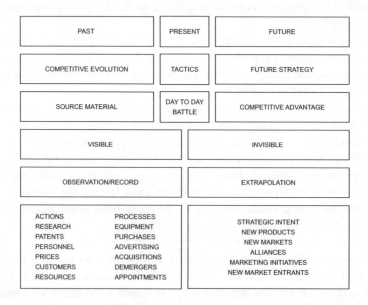

Figure 5 *The CI situation*

straightforward since a high proportion of what happened there is visible. Its importance is that it shows the evolution of competitors' activities and provides source material for making projections.

The time dimension in which a high proportion of competitive intelligence activity is focused is the present. Here the intelligence is tactical in nature and is used in the day-to-day struggle with competitors. Much of it is visible but may also involve short-term projections to make it more useful.

The fundamental objectives of competitive intelligence are to avoid surprises and gain competitive advantage. These can be achieved only if future actions by competitors can be predicted accurately. Forward-looking, strategic intelligence is easier to discuss than it is to obtain. Direct evidence of overall future strategy may exist in management statements but intelligence on the methods by which the strategy will be implemented is invariably fragmentary. It can however be inferred from in-depth analysis of competitors, by long-term tracking of the actions they take and by studying the personalities and objectives of the management that run them. However, this type of analysis is good only for as long as the past is a guide to what competitors will do in the future. The analysis must also take account of major changes in ownership, structure and management that may result in changes in objectives and changes in the way in which competitors respond to the market environment.

Note

1. Jan Herring, 'Key Intelligence Topics: A Process to Identify and Define Intelligence Needs', *Competitive Intelligence Review*, vol. 10, no. 2, Second Quarter 1999, pp. 4–14.

5 Overview of the Sources of Intelligence

Competitive intelligence can be obtained from a wide variety of sources. Some of the sources are obvious but many are obscure. Some are easy to use or access, others are extremely difficult or uncooperative. The key skills in all competitive intelligence are the ability to identify the sources that are likely to have the data that are required and the ability to extract them. At its simplest competitive intelligence can involve scanning the national and trade press for news items on competitors and maintaining a watch on their websites. At its most complex it could involve direct interrogation of competitors' staff. The route that is chosen will depend largely on the data that are required, the importance attached to having access to the intelligence, the time and physical resources that are available and the budget. Needless to say, complex intelligence-gathering exercises tend to use more resources than those that have more straightforward objectives, though there is always scope for surprises. Seemingly simple intelligence objectives can sometimes prove unusually difficult to fulfil.

Primary and Secondary Sources

The basic division of intelligence sources, as in many other types of research, is:

- Secondary sources containing information in the public domain
- Primary sources

As shown in Figure 6, both secondary and primary sources can exist within and outside the company.

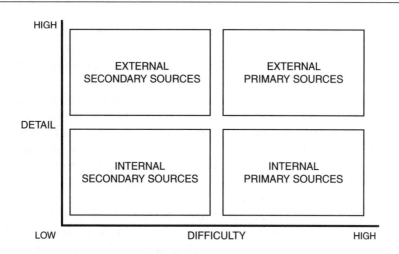

Figure 6 *The basic building blocks*

Secondary sources of intelligence are defined as those that are publicly available. This does not mean that they are readily available, only that they are deemed to be in the 'public domain' and can be accessed by anyone who can make the effort to do so. As will be shown, there are a wide variety of secondary sources, many of which are easy to identify and some that take considerable time and ingenuity to locate. All competitor analysts rely heavily on secondary sources. For some they are the only permitted sources of information. Companies that have an above-average sensitivity to antitrust or other legislation on competition regard the use of any information that cannot be collected from publicly available sources as being risky if not outright dangerous. This obviously limits the depth to which they can probe but still leaves them with rich veins of intelligence to mine.

Secondary sources are published or held in databases. They include all types of written publications and on-line or disk databases which either report or store information on companies and the business sectors in which they operate. With the notable exception of published reports, secondary sources are generally inexpensive to access and consult. The main requirement is time.

Secondary sources exist within and outside the company and it is normally preferable to exhaust the internal sources before embarking on any external search. Within companies secondary sources may be held in databases, records or libraries but they are just as likely to be held by individuals in their own personal filing systems. Traditionally external secondary sources were found in locations such as public reference libraries or trade associations. However, the Internet has revolutionised the access to secondary intelligence. A high proportion of, though far from all, relevant intelligence is no more than a few taps on a keyboard away. No longer does the intelligence seeker need to rely on the buying policy of the local or national reference libraries or on the willingness of companies to send brochures and annual reports. The Internet and its powerful search engines have short-circuited the entire search and collection process, whilst at the same time making available intelligence from increasingly esoteric and previously unknown sources.

Primary sources are mainly people who are in a position to impart intelligence about companies when questioned. They also include direct observations of competitors' activities on the ground, from the air or even by satellite. As with secondary sources, the people that have intelligence on competitors include those employed by the company seeking the intelligence as well as those working externally.

There is no limit to the people from which intelligence can be obtained, providing they can be identified and contacted within an acceptable timeframe. The most valuable sources are those that have direct experience of competitors' operations. These include the staff of competitor companies and the staff of companies that work with them or have some form of business relationship. The latter include suppliers, distributors, advisers and customers. Sources that are less direct but also potentially valuable include the staff of organisations whose role provides them with opportunities to observe the activities of competitors. These include analysts, journalists, consultants, trade association staff, the staff of Chambers of Commerce and other observers of businesses at a national or local level.

Determinants of Methods Used

The key determinants of the mix of intelligence-gathering techniques that are deployed are:

- The characteristics of the intelligence required
- The depth and detail of intelligence being sought
- The frequency at which intelligence will be collected
- The manpower available
- The time that is available
- The budget available

The characteristics of the intelligence required

As will be shown in subsequent chapters, considerable amounts of intelligence are available from secondary sources. It is frequently possible to fulfil straightforward intelligence briefs by doing little more than scanning the daily press and trade literature, reviewing brochures, downloading data off competitors' websites and analysing published financial statements. Sophisticated intelligence users are rarely satisfied by data derived from such sources, but it is wrong to assume that all requirements require more than a rigorous secondary search.

Nevertheless, secondary sources tend to suffer from a number of deficiencies that are often severe enough to propel intelligence users towards primary sources. The main weakness is that secondary data are available to all who choose to collect them and although there is room for approaches and interpretations that are more creative than others, there is no clear opportunity to obtain intelligence that is proprietary or unique. Furthermore, the companies themselves, through press releases, analysts' briefings, brochures and websites, supply much of the flow of data that can be obtained from secondary sources. Although control of the data is far from perfect, there is ample opportunity to insert contradictions and biases that can mislead those studying their activities. Secondary data also suffer from the fact that they are normally published after a time delay and lack immediacy.

The depth and detail of intelligence being sought

For wholly understandable reasons, data from published sources will commonly be lacking detail and open to a number of different interpretations. Financial statements from companies rarely report sales at less than a divisional or product category level, leaving the details to be guessed at. Reports on the reasons for actions taken are couched in generalities rather than specifics. Similarly, plans are described in outline terms leaving out any details of how they could be achieved. Lists of contracts and clients are usually partial rather than complete.

If an overview is all that is required a profile based on secondary sources may be adequate; however, when it is important to know details, secondary source analysis needs to be supplemented by primary research.

The frequency at which intelligence will be collected

Tracking competitors' activities poses particular problems for primary research approaches that are not shared by secondary sources. The examination of secondary sources is invisible to the staff of the target company itself. Primary contacts are not and whilst it is normally possible to make successful direct contacts for a limited amount of time, any sustained programme of calling will ultimately draw attention to the fact that the company is being studied. Normally this results in attempts to eliminate the outflow of information by means of instructions to staff to refuse to answer questions from outsiders. All competitive intelligence gatherers have experienced a shutdown, the point at which it becomes evident that respondents are suspicious and will no longer answer questions, and it normally happens when they have been pushing their luck and calling too frequently.

Although there are multiple sources of information within and outside companies, long-term intelligence programmes need to use primary research techniques sparingly or innovatively in order to remain below the threshold of activity that will set alarm bells ringing.

Manpower available

The choice of techniques is critically dependent on the resources that can be committed to intelligence gathering. In the relatively rare cases in which competitive intelligence is a major activity, teams of analysts are available to collect raw data, interpret them and disseminate the results to those who will use them. However, a high proportion of intelligence users rely on a single staff member to carry out all parts of the intelligence process. Although they may be able to coopt other staff members into the intelligence programme for specific assignments, there are severe limits on what they can be expected to achieve.

Small internal intelligence teams tend to rely on a limited range of secondary sources which over time have been shown to be the most fruitful and the most cost-effective to access. They may extend the range of their intelligence gathering by briefing and debriefing the company's sales and marketing staff, especially when an industry exhibition or conference brings them into contact with the staff of competitors. For more extensive programmes they rely on a budget being made available to employ external intelligence gatherers.

The time that is available

In all research, time is as important a resource as manpower and budget. This is particularly true in competitive intelligence where information on competitors' activities that have already happened has already lost a high proportion of its usefulness. The premium on timeliness can restrict the intelligence-gathering approach to those research activities that can be carried out quickly or to a monitoring process that ensures that all useful items are collected immediately they are reported.

Although secondary sources can be consulted quickly, especially when available on the Internet, primary intelligence-gathering approaches require more time to set up and complete. Apart from planning and set-up time they depend on the availability of people to speak to. Key information sources cannot be accessed at will and it can take several days, if not weeks, to track them down, penetrate voicemail systems and overcome defensive secretaries and personal assistants.

Budget availability

Intelligence costs money but some approaches cost more than others. Primary intelligence gathering is rarely cheap, even when carried out by internal resources, largely because they take longer to complete and require higher levels of skill. Companies that place a high value on accurate and timely competitive intelligence are usually prepared to allocate sufficient budget to ensure that the most productive approaches can be used.

6

Secondary Sources of Intelligence

As explained in the previous chapter, secondary sources are normally the first to be consulted in intelligence-gathering programmes. They vary in usefulness, timeliness and accuracy but they represent a relatively low-cost and sometimes a reasonably comprehensive method of acquiring intelligence.

This chapter is not intended to provide a detailed listing of sources. Such guides do exist and are referred to in the text where applicable. The intention is to provide a reasonably complete description of generic groups of sources, thereby showing the directions in which researchers should be aiming their efforts. Even this limited objective will be difficult to achieve given the variety of sources that exist. Many sources are specific to industry sectors and using the guidelines set out in this chapter it will be the reader's task to locate them for themselves.

Internal Intelligence Sources

The first sources to be consulted should be those that are available within the company. Even organisations that have not invested in a corporate library will have amassed a wealth of information about their competitors. The problem is finding it.

The intelligence audit

The intelligence audit is a process for discovering the intelligence that is available from internal sources. It regards intelligence as a key corporate asset that needs to be identified and put to work just like any other physical asset the company has invested in. The main difference between intelligence and physical assets is that the company has not always made a conscious decision to acquire intelligence. Much of what is valuable has been obtained as a by-product of other activities, such as selling, and resides in various parts of the organisation, not in some central repository where it can be easily accessed. The objectives of an audit are to:

- Identify all sources and potential sources of intelligence within the company
- Categorise the intelligence by type, relevance and quality
- Collect and examine the intelligence that they can provide
- Establish the sources from which the intelligence was obtained
- Check the credentials of the sources (are they qualified to provide the intelligence?)
- Check the veracity of the intelligence
- Establish whether the intelligence can be updated or extended

The audit should cover fixed and renewable sources of intelligence. Fixed sources include one-off documents, books, files and reports that have been compiled or commissioned. They provide intelligence covering a finite period of time. Their usefulness decays from the moment they are completed until such time as they become completely out of date and worth retaining for historical reasons only. As, over time, new fixed sources become available, they need to be added to the available resource.

Renewable sources of intelligence are those which are automatically updated. They include data feeds, subscriptions to journals and the trade press, on-line databases and competitor websites. They offer the ability to update the intelligence on competitors' activities on a regular basis or when a special analysis is required.

The following types of internal sources should be included in the intelligence audit.

Library files

Not all companies have them but where a corporate information officer or a company librarian exists they are likely to be a significant source of intelligence. In the course of providing an information service covering all types of information required to operate the company, information officers invariably collect a wealth of information about the companies that are active in the company's business sector. It is impossible to run an effective information centre without being highly organised and the information that is collected should therefore be easily accessible in files and databases.

A good company library should carry all official statistics covering the business in which the company operates, trade statistics, company annual reports, other official filings made by competitor companies and brokers' reports on those of the competitors whose shares are publicly traded.

Market research reports

Although commissioned for purposes other than competitive intelligence, market research reports can contain useful data. Typically they can include:

- Market share analysis
- Distribution channels used by competitors
- Key accounts of competitors
- Customer satisfaction with competitors
- An analysis of customers' perceptions of the strengths and weaknesses of competitors' products and service levels

Staff files

Staff with an outward-facing role often keep files of information which they have collected for their personal or general use. These files commonly cover the market and the competitors active within it and are likely to include competitors' brochures and catalogues, press clippings, newsletters, promotional pieces, notices of appointments, copies of annual reports and other official filings, brokers' reports and other privately compiled reports on competitors.

Other functions that could carry information on competitors are research and development and production staff. R&D could keep files of patents registered by competitors and articles describing competitors' technologies. Production staff may collect information about the production equipment and processes used by competitors, either gleaned directly from discussions with fellow production staff or from sales representatives promoting their products on the basis that they are used by competitors.

Trade association reports and statistics

Membership of an industry or trade association offers a significant benefit for competitive intelligence in the form of reports and statistics. It also provides a forum in which competitors can be met officially (about which more later). Trade association statistics show the total sales of members and may provide evidence of the sales of individual suppliers. Reports show the general state of the business, analyse trends and provide news of members.

Sales representatives' reports

Sales representatives have direct and indirect contact with the staff of competitors. They often know their opposite numbers in competitor companies and also hear about competitors' activities from customers. The sales reporting process can therefore provide trade gossip about competitors, intelligence on competitors' sales and technical staff, leavers and joiners, the reasons why competitors are winning or losing business, new product developments, product and service problems and the culture within competitive organisations.

External Secondary Sources

Internal secondary sources are likely to have their limits. Unless carefully orchestrated by an efficient intelligence officer who has been working to a plan of intelligence requirements, they are likely to be patchy in their coverage and biased towards the specific interests of those collecting the data. This does not invalidate their usefulness but means that they must be supplemented by reference to external sources. As hinted several times, there are vast arrays of sources that can be consulted, though, as most researchers will admit, this can be an intensely frustrating exercise. It is essential that the coverage of potential sources of intelligence is comprehensive but at the same time the amount of intelligence that is extracted from each source may be little or none. Sifting through articles in endless issues of trade magazines may yield no useful intelligence but is carried on in the hope that a nugget of information is eventually located. The frustration is heightened by the fact that the task cannot be delegated to junior staff since they may not recognise useful intelligence. The intelligence mind must be trained to think along the lines, 'if I cannot find the exact data I am seeking, what is the closest I can get, what will act as a surrogate or are there some overall data that will enable me to make an informed guess?'

Official company filings

The most direct intelligence on competitors is gained from sources prepared and published by themselves for statutory reporting or for promotional purposes. No company can be silent about its activities and although most are fully aware that their documents will fall into the hands of their competitors there is nothing they can do to conceal their activities without jeopardising their chances of winning business or falling foul of the authorities.

The official filings are generally well-known and are invariably on the shopping lists of competitor analysts. Their usefulness varies from country to country but the extent to which they can distort the facts is minimal even though the amount they reveal can be controlled.

The key sources to be collected and examined are the following.

Annual reports and accounts

All limited liability companies must produce an annual set of audited accounts for tax purposes and to comply with legal reporting requirements. These comprise a minimum of a directors' report, a profit and loss account, a balance sheet, an auditor's report, notes to the accounts, the allotment of shares and the ultimate holding company. Depending on the country, the reporting requirements may be extended to include a list of directors showing their date of appointment, home address, nationality and other directorships held. These data are particularly useful for tracing relationships between companies.

There is a significant difference regarding the information that is available between public and private companies. The former have to conform to regulations on disclosure, which force them to reveal considerable amounts of information about their activities to their various stakeholders, particularly in the USA. The reporting requirements for privately owned companies are less onerous and although in Europe private companies must file accounts with various national and local agencies, in the USA they do not.

Copies of reports and accounts can be obtained from the companies themselves or from the relevant authority with which they are filed. In the UK this is Companies House but in other European countries the reports may be filed either with a national authority or with a local body in the region in which the company is registered. Obtaining copies of private company reports and accounts may require a visit to the location at which the accounts are held.

Stock exchange and SEC filings

Quoted companies must produce an annual report to shareholders, which includes statements about the company's business, its trading performance and its future prospects as well as a full set of accounts. The annual reports are in part sales documents designed to maintain the company's share price but, depending on the company, they can provide considerable insight into its activities by product line or by division. The published glossy reports on European companies tend to be fairly full in their coverage whereas in the United States they are little more than a chairman's statement, basic accounts and a lot of colour photographs. However, US-quoted companies must also file annual 10-Ks and quarterly 10-Qs with the Securities Exchange Commission.[1] These reveal considerably more information than that contained in the average European annual report. Typically, in addition to detailed financial information, they include:

- Company history
- Profiles of the key executives
- The markets in which the company is operating
- A statement on competition
- A review of trading conditions
- Product developments
- Properties
- Acquisitions
- Sales of assets
- Remuneration and pension schemes

The 10-Qs provide quarterly financial data and an abbreviated version of the data contained in the 10-K filings.

Additional information must be made available to shareholders when major changes to the company's business are proposed. The most common event is an acquisition, which places an obligation on the acquirer to state why the acquisition is proposed and on the target company to state why a bid should be accepted or rejected. Major defence operations yield considerably more information than uncontested bids, much of which finds its way into the financial press for easy access.

Companies are of course aware that the most avid readers of their annual reports and other filings are their competitors. They may therefore seek to minimise the damage by being as vague as the regulations will permit and disperse information so that it is difficult to pull together a complete picture. This must be done with care since the readers for which reports are really intended are the shareholders and their advisers and by being over-zealous in trying to protect information they may also create an unfavourable impression of the company and have an adverse effect on their share price.

Prospectuses

Prior to a new public issue of shares or a private placement, companies must issue a prospectus. This is a legal document drawn up by the company and its advisers and provides a statement of the company's business in sufficient depth to inform potential or current shareholders about the nature and value of the investment and the risks to which investors are exposed. A prospectus is also a sales document but it cannot contain misleading statements. They are normally available at the office at which the company is registered and can be obtained from the company itself or its financial adviser.

Planning applications

Planning applications must be made for all new premises and extensions to existing premises. Critical subjects for planning authorities are the effects of an application on the local environment, pollution, waste water, refuse, the processes to be used and the equipment to be installed. The extent to which detailed planning applications are published varies from country to country but where obtainable they provide direct evidence of competitors' production plans and capacities.

Company documents

Promotional documents, technical data sheets and directory entries provide detailed intelligence on competitors' products and services. Since their primary audience is customers their accuracy is virtually guaranteed though it is often necessary to cut through a level of hyperbole in order to access the facts. The main documents that can be obtained are the following.

Brochures

Brochures provide the standard descriptions of products and product families that are available from suppliers. They can contain detailed technical information and performance data plus a description of the support services and service levels that are provided. They may also contain reference data on past clients in the form of lists or endorsements.

Catalogues

Catalogues are useful for obtaining information on the product ranges that are available from competitors and the key parameters of each product type.

Directories, buyers' guides and exhibition catalogues

Directories and buyers' guides are useful as sources on products available from all or most of the suppliers active in a market. Their accuracy depends on the care with which they are compiled and the frequency at which they are revised. Directories must always be treated with caution. Entries based on forms completed by companies themselves commonly exaggerate the range of products they offer whereas those for which payment is required to enter will rarely be comprehensive.

The catalogues from exhibitions will also contain omissions to the extent that companies choose not to exhibit. The entries are nevertheless useful since they tend to describe the new products or technologies currently of interest to the supplier and therefore on display.

Company house journals and newsletters

House journals and newsletters are intended for customers and employees and are a means of disseminating information about the company, new products being launched, new processes being used, changes in the organisational structure, profiles of key managers, new appointments (from within and from outside), office moves and new manufacturing and warehousing locations. Success stories commonly feature in these publications thereby providing intelligence on the identity of and relationship with key customers. The personnel-related items can provide intelligence about the culture prevailing within the company.

House journals can also carry articles that provide managers' perspectives on the development of their business and the issues that they consider are important now and in the future. Whilst these may be billed as personal views rather than official company policy they nevertheless provide insight into the thinking within the organisation, which may ultimately influence company actions.

Regulatory authority reports

Industries that are regulated, notably those that were formerly in government ownership or are deemed to be in need of regulation in the public interest, are subject to frequent reviews. Whilst these reviews are normally designed to highlight the role (and success) of the regulatory agency itself, the reports can contain data on the level of activity in the sector and the performance of the regulated companies. The sectors that are most frequently subject to regulation are:

- Telecommunications
- Transport
- Power utilities
- Water

Brokers' reports

The analysts working in stockbrokers' research departments and competitive intelligence analysts are kindred spirits. Although the reasons for their research are different much of the output is similar. Stockbrokers' analysts cover only quoted companies and are biased towards a financial evaluation. However, they have to take into account product ranges and new product development, new production technologies, the market and competition in order to draw conclusions about future earnings levels. Their main usefulness to competitive intelligence analysts is that their reports are based on briefings they receive from companies. They are also able to question the corporate staff. The reports they issue to investors and the recommendations they make regarding the future of share prices and whether they should be purchased, sold or held, are of vital interest to the companies themselves. Investor relations departments and company secretaries are therefore highly motivated to provide them with information and it is rare for them to issue statements that are misleading. Brokers' reports are easy to obtain and since it is common for a number of analysts to follow the same company there is usually a selection to draw from.

Credit reporting agencies

The reports issued by credit reporting agencies, such as Dun & Bradstreet, are of greatest value when dealing with private companies. Credit reports are designed to reassure suppliers and clients that the company is safe to deal with. They analyse companies' payment records by questioning a sample of suppliers. The data can often provide advanced warnings of cash or trading problems when payments become stretched.

Whereas they may add little to the information that is publicly available on public companies, for private companies they are frequently able to provide sales information not contained in other sources, ownership details and management comments on performance.

Financial databases

Examples of these are the financial databases held by Dun & Bradstreet and its various worldwide subsidiaries and national sources such as ICC and Jordans in the UK. Financial databases are of most use in screening companies. The depth of information they provide is limited but their coverage can be massive.

Company histories

Company histories appear as one-off books commissioned by the companies themselves, in pamphlets issued by public relations departments and in compendiums, such as the International Directory of Company Histories which covers over 2500 companies. The origins and development of a company can have a defining influence on current strategy if only through the culture that has been instilled as a result.

Published media

Published media of all types are a key source for competitive intelligence. Their main value is that they carry a large amount of information and that it is relatively timely. The disadvantage is that news coverage is rarely comprehensive, can be heavily influenced by companies themselves and when it appears in the press it is available to everybody.

The national and local press

Newspapers and journals provide coverage of a broad spectrum of company and business news including:

• All types of news events relating to individual companies
• Commentaries on companies' performance
• Industry-wide information and reviews

- Technical developments
- Information on, and profiles of, management
- Joiners and leavers
- Job opportunities
- Legal notices published to comply with local laws and regulations

The articles are drawn from news items released by companies themselves, interviews, investigations, technical and conference papers and commentaries prepared by journalists and others with an interest in the business. Large quoted companies receive a disproportional amount of coverage in the national press, but smaller companies can be of equal interest to the local press servicing the communities in which they operate.

The financial press, such as the *Financial Times* and the *Wall Street Journal*, is of particular interest for competitive intelligence since it focuses on the activities of companies.

Business journals

Key business journals, such as *The Economist, Fortune, Forbes* and *Business Week*, and to a lesser extent the news journals, such as *Time*, are all likely to contain items covering the affairs of specific companies. They are most likely to appear in such journals when they have done something extraordinary or have suffered some grave misfortune, events which are also likely to have picked up by the national and trade press. Nevertheless, there is a chance that their more investigative approach to journalism will uncover facts not reported in the daily press.

The trade press

There are trade press magazines covering almost every business. Some are relatively general and others are highly specific. The only criteria that determine whether there is a viable opportunity for a trade magazine are the number of potential readers and the number of potential advertisers wishing to reach them. If the advertising revenues that can be obtained cover the costs and yield an adequate profit, then a magazine is likely to be produced. Once launched, trade magazines need a continuous flow of news, feature articles and editorial matter and act as a magnet to the news stories emanating from companies. They can therefore be counted upon to record most of the significant events in the sectors they cover.

Trade magazines fall into three categories, all of which need to be covered in competitive intelligence exercises. The first are those devoted to a particular business sector. These are the most specialised but are likely to record all that happens in the sector in the way of product launches, company events, sector events (such as trade shows and exhibitions) and the movement of people. The second are manufacturing technique-related, such as welding or process control, and cover developments in the technique in all industry sectors that use it. The third are subject-related, such as marketing, advertising or human relations, and cover the subject as it applies to all manufacturing and service sectors. Articles containing competitive intelligence can appear in all three types of magazine.

Professional journals

Professional journals are the official publications of professional societies. The articles they publish tend to be more 'worthy' than those in the trade press and are accepted on the basis that they advance professional knowledge and practice. However, many of the members of professional societies are working in companies and the articles they write often expose internal company practices.

Academic and semi-academic publications

The academic press, such as the *Harvard Business Review*, and semi-academic journals such as the *McKinsey Quarterly*, published by the consultancy company, frequently contain case studies relating to the use of management techniques by companies and interviews with management about how their companies are run. The insights these can provide into the strategic directions being pursued by the subject companies are sometimes substantially more enlightening than those providing the information intended.

Industry newsletters

Industry newsletters are commonly a compendium of information on a business sector derived from secondary sources. Although they may contain original information, their main use is as a short-cut to what is generally available in other sources.

Conference papers

Most of the papers delivered at conferences organised for industry sectors and on business topics are by people working in companies. The papers are normally based on their working experience and, when studied carefully, can often yield company intelligence.

Contract listings

In some industries contracts to be placed and contracts won are listed in specialist journals. The *Official Journal* published daily by the European Community provides insight into where government contracts are being placed and a number of privately published sources cover the construction, civil engineering and mechanical engineering sectors.

Government statistics and reports

Governments worldwide are not only major users of information; they also collect it on a vast scale. They do so for a variety of reasons, which include the needs of government departments to perform their functions, the need to prove that government is doing a good job and the need to provide a service to their various constituents. The fact that some information collection is politically motivated does not necessarily detract from its usefulness, though it may suggest that it should be examined carefully before it is accepted as being completely accurate.

Information collected by governments ranges from statistical enquiries, mainly covering production, distribution and trade, to in-depth investigations of industry sectors, business practices and corporate activity. Governments also collect information and report on the economic performance of their countries as a basis for deciding on economic policy and the measures to be taken to control economic growth and inflation.

For competitive intelligence the main interest arises from the fact that all governments assume responsibility for regulating the activities of companies and are keenly interested in any activities that threaten competition. The two instances in which a government enquiry can be of most assistance to competitive intelligence analysts is when a company or an industry sector is investigated for monopolistic practices or price fixing and when a proposed merger is investigated for fear that it will create a monopoly. References to competition authorities, either national or international, are feared by the companies involved not only because of the delays and the large amounts of staff time such investigations can absorb but also because of the amounts of information that are disclosed when the final reports are published.

Venture capital reports

Venture capitalists provide finance for start-ups, young developing companies and management buy-outs. The detailed financial arrangements between a venture capitalist and its investments are normally secret but the industry is subject to constant scrutiny and reports are published on the activities of companies in which investments have been made and contain an outline of deals that have been concluded. Analysis of these reports can provide advance warning of interesting new technologies and potential acquisition candidates when the venture capitalist is seeking to exit from its investment.

Trade association reports

Trade associations are commonly formed as a meeting point and as a vehicle for lobbying government on industry matters. They also provide a service to their members by collecting statistics and commissioning reports. Trade association statistics normally cover:

- Aggregate sales by members broken down by key product types and market sectors
- Growth in sales, month on month and year on year
- Average wage and salary levels by types of employee

The statistics provide measurements of activity from which members can derive their overall market shares, their success in the various segments of the market, the extent to which their own growth has matched that of the business as a whole and their competitiveness in the job market. The published statistics may need to be adjusted to allow for companies that are not members or have chosen not to report, but they are usually more accurate than sample surveys.

Associations may also provide more qualitative assessments of trading conditions and news on developments by member companies.

Published market research reports

The market research business offers a wide range of products of use to the competitive intelligence analyst. These can be categorised as follows:

- Panel surveys, which track the sales of products through retail channels and purchases by various categories of households or customers; unlike the trade association statistics these normally show the estimated market shares of each supplier
- Published reports on products or industry sectors; these usually contain intelligence on the structure of the business, market share analysis and the activities of the major suppliers active within it

Patent databases

Patent applications provide a leading indication of new technologies and the directions in which companies are channelling their research and development investment. Before the advent of patent databases, such as Derwent's World Patent Index and a host of specialist patent monitors, keeping track on competitors' patent applications and patents granted was a laborious process made complex by the fact that patent filings are required in each country or region in which patent protection is to be sought. To track the patent situation fully required the use of specialist investigators. The patent databases have simplified the process considerably as has the Europe-wide patent agency established in the early 1990s.

Patents show a number of items of value to those tracking product development including:

• The inventor
• The identity of any company licensed to use the patent
• The characteristics of the invention
• How the invention works
• Citations

Patents place developments in the public domain but provide the inventor with legal protection against any infringements. Companies do not always seek patent protection for their developments particularly if they feel there is a risk the patent will not be granted.

Satellite observation

Satellite images are being actively sold for competitive intelligence by a number of vendors.[2] High-resolution digital satellite images can show:

• Plant layout
• External processes
• Transport facilities
• External stocks
• New plant construction

Images can also be used to track changes month by month or year by year. Current satellite technology can show objects down to the size of a large lawnmower.

Locating External Secondary Intelligence

Secondary intelligence is physically located in three types of sources:

- Libraries
- Databases
- The Internet

Libraries

Despite the rapid rise in electronic communications the old-fashioned library is still a useful repository of intelligence. Once entered, scanning library shelves can be quicker than searching the Internet and depending on the skills of the librarian and the budget they have access to, the human search engine can still locate rich veins of intelligence.

The libraries that are most valuable are:

- National reference libraries, such as the British Library, the Library of Congress and the Export Marketing Intelligence Centre at the Department of Trade and Industry
- Specialist libraries, such as the East European library
- Government department libraries
- University libraries, particularly those with business schools
- Institute libraries, such as that of the Institute of Mechanical Engineers
- Trade association libraries
- Research association libraries
- Company libraries

The main disadvantage of libraries is that they have to be accessed physically which can entail a long and expensive journey. Their advantage is that they often contain obscure sources that will never find their way on to the Internet.

Access to libraries, particularly those set up for the use of an organisation's members, staff or students, may prove to be a problem but the library community tends to be one in which there is considerable sharing of resources. It is therefore possible that a source not held in a local reference library can be obtained on loan from another library that stocks it. Special visitor permits to use a library that is normally closed to outsiders may also be available on request or for the payment of a small fee.

Databases

Since the 1980s there has been a growing trend to collect data into proprietary databases, which are available either on-line or on CD-Roms for efficient and rapid searching. Host organisations running on-line services have a strong financial incentive to expand the range of information they carry and owners of information are equally interested in expanding their customer base by adding on-line channels to their conventional methods of distribution. Although many databases are still available on CD-Roms, they are more difficult to update than the on-line versions and their main application is for intelligence that has a lasting value.

The key types of competitive intelligence that can be collected more efficiently by database searches are:

- Local, national and international news items
- Trade press items
- Business and professional journals
- Company financial information
- Information on mergers and acquisitions
- Government information
- Economic data
- Patents
- Citations
- Trademarks
- Scientific and technical information
- Medical and healthcare literature
- Legal information
- Tax information
- Information on currency
- Share prices
- Biographies of businessmen and businesswomen

There are an increasing number of guides to the sources listed above, such as Findex, and magazine indexes are available on-line that offer the potential to identify useful studies and articles efficiently, even if the documents themselves have to be obtained in hard copy.

Proprietary databases are available only to subscribers or those who pay as they go for their use. Annual subscriptions can be quite high, commonly in the range of £5000 to £6000, and it is worth subscribing only if the use that will be made of them will be sufficient to justify the cost. Other routes can source much of the more general intelligence contained in the databases and their main justification is the time that using a database will save.

The Internet

The Internet is rapidly becoming the 'method of choice' for secondary intelligence searches. The fact that its coverage is global, that the data that can be accessed through it are extraordinarily diverse and expanding at a phenomenal rate and that it is thought to be largely free tempts analysts to seek the entirety of their secondary intelligence requirements through the Internet. The use of the Internet as a competitive intelligence tool is covered fully in Chapter 7 but it is important to remember that it still has limits both in content and in terms of the efficiency at which searches can be carried out.

Notes

1. Easily accessible on the SEC's website which hosts the EDGAR database. The web address is www.sec.gov.
2. See Fred Wergeles, 'Commercial Satellite Imagery – New Opportunities for Competitive Intelligence', *Competitive Intelligence Magazine*, vol. 1, no. 1, April–June 1998, pp. 36–9.

7 Intelligence on the Internet

The Internet has revolutionised the search for information. Data that once took weeks to acquire can now be available at a few clicks of a mouse. This applies to all types of information but those seeking intelligence on competitors have been particular beneficiaries of the Internet revolution. The number of websites put up by companies and devoted to news about the activities of companies is disproportionately large. It is rare to find a company of any significance that does not have a website on which it posts a description of its activities, its facilities, its product range, its partners, press releases, technical papers, job opportunities and contact points. The wealth of information available on even the most basic sites is far in excess of that which could be obtained from hard-copy brochures and catalogues and directory entries.

The web has become the primary route to all of the intelligence sources outlined in Chapter 6. However, the Internet is not without its problems. Those who promote the web as a vast store of free information are not far from the truth, at least in areas where local telephone calls are free and if the measure is volume rather than value. The main problem is that a high proportion of the free information on the Internet is useless for business purposes and it takes considerable amounts of time and ingenuity to sift through it to get to items that are relevant. The second problem is that volume rarely equates to quality. Research on the market for peanut butter will identify hundreds of sites providing recipes for peanut butter cookies, some telling the history of the peanut, some recording the size of the peanut crop worldwide, a large number of sites outlining the services of peanut wholesalers and very, very few giving any statistics on peanut butter consumption.

Although, as stated above, a high proportion of the data available from the web is free of charge, the most valuable information is not.

The web has to be seen not only as a means of accessing intelligence but also as a method by which those who sell intelligence can deliver it to their clients. Many of the more useful sources charge for their intelligence and buying it on the web is simply quicker and more convenient than placing an order and waiting for hard copy.

The only rule of the game on the Internet is to be prepared to be surprised – both ways. Sometimes the simplest item of information proves incredibly difficult to locate whilst on other occasions a highly esoteric topic may be covered in great depth. Making sense of what is available on the Internet is far from easy and many of the guides that have been written are more confusing than enlightening. This is partly due to the fact that because of its diversity and scale it is impossible to classify easily. The purpose of this chapter is not to list all that can be found on the Internet but to describe that which is unique to the web and its use as a means of accessing secondary intelligence. Although some sites are mentioned the reader will have to look elsewhere for specific listings of all that is available on the web.[1]

Search Engines and Web Crawlers

The most common way of identifying information on the web is to use the powerful search engines that have been developed specifically for this purpose. Most researchers start with the tried and tested engines, such as Yahoo, Lycos, Excite, Go (formerly Infoseek) and Alta Vista, that have an area of coverage defined by their search algorithms. However, none of these search engines can offer complete coverage of the web and to broaden the scope of the search it is necessary to use several engines. This adds to the time taken to search and can be avoided by using 'web crawlers'. These make use of a number of search engines to complete their task. Useful web crawlers are Google, Metacrawler and Webcrawler, all of which make use of the standard search engines listed above and extend the coverage of a search considerably.

One of the main problems with conventional search engines is their inability to search effectively using complex search criteria. Some, such as Go, permit sequential searches within searches that make it possible to zero in on specific topics but the results are still relatively broadly based. The latest generation of search engines uses a 'natural language query system' that accepts direct questions rather than strings of words. The best known is Ask Jeeves, which is heavily promoted for personal users of the web. Less well known but more tailored to searches for business intelligence are Elfsoft, nQuire, English Query and English Wizard. In addition to the web, natural language query systems can also be used to interrogate databases as a replacement for the more complex SQL and are likely to be encountered more frequently as database providers seek to make their offers more user friendly.

Hard copy web 'yellow pages' are available to supplement the search engines. Some of them have added value features such as comments on sites. Their main disadvantage is that they are not published frequently enough to keep pace with the growth of the web. This is not quite as damning as it may seem, since the introduction of sites which can make a major contribution to competitive intelligence is nowhere near as rapid as the growth in the web as a whole, but it can mean that some interesting sites lie unrecorded for a period of time.

Intelligence Content of the Web

Despite its size the web is particularly good for some types of intelligence and next to useless for others. The web shines as a method of accessing any intelligence that is published in the press, journals, company documents, market reports, government reports, conference proceedings and exhibition guides. It also contains facilities to locate and communicate with highly specialised communities by tapping into discussions on topics that have specific intelligence applications and by reaching targeted groups of individuals to ask for intelligence.

The most useful and most used published content of the web includes:

- Press articles
- Newswires
- On-line databases
- Market reports
- Company news
- Financial data
- Company websites
- Recruitment
- Research reports
- Industry statistics
- Economic and demographic data
- Other government data
- Conference and trade shows

Press articles

The web can be used to access vast databases of press articles thereby eliminating the time-consuming searches that used to be the case when hard copy was all that was available. These databases exist in a number of different forms, namely:

- Company websites on which press releases are posted
- Newspapers, trade press, magazines and journals that are published (and sometimes indexed) on the web as well as in hard copy
- Indexing and abstracting services covering specialist topics
- Articles published on the web and accessible by the search engines

Most of the major national newspapers now have a website that hosts the current and back issues of their publications. This makes backtracking for information relatively easy. Access to local newspapers and the trade press is more limited but, where it exists, no less useful.

Some newspapers, most notably the *Financial Times*, have broadened their business base to include major on-line databases that can be searched by subscribers, as have some of the more specialised broadcast channels such as CNN and Bloomberg.

Using services that filter stories according to criteria set by the analyst can facilitate searching the news media. Companysleuth.com can provide a daily feed of stories referring to selected companies, thus eliminating the need to search each site manually. Northern Lights is a favourite with analysts as a rapid route to news stories on companies.

Newswires

Newswires are services to the media that distribute news items filed with them by originators, such as company public relations departments, or developed by their own correspondents or stringers. The major newswire services have been around since the main method of distributing news was by telegraph. They include names familiar to any newspaper reader such as Reuters, Associated Press, United Press, Agence France Press and the Press Association as well as government press agencies. The newswires no longer rely entirely on the media for income and have opened up their services to anyone willing to pay for access to their comprehensive databases of news stories.

On-line databases

Databases can be accessed in three ways – on CD-Roms, by direct dial-up and via the Internet. As far as most users are concerned the convenience of on-line databases has enabled them to supersede CD-Roms and direct dialling as means of gaining access to databases though the older methods still have a role to fulfil. Those that have access to major public and university libraries may still find CD-Roms the lowest-cost method of accessing data. Others may prefer them because they do not incur communication costs, are free from the delay problems still inherent in using the Internet and are often a less expensive source of data even when purchased outright. Direct dialling provides much faster access to data but requires knowledge of the protocols and language used by each database.

However accessed, the subscription charges to on-line databases can be substantial and justified only if the use to be made of them is heavy.

The key on-line databases that can be considered for competitive intelligence are:

- Dun & Bradstreet – financial databases
- Disclosure
- Investext
- Dialog (Profound)
- Lexis (legal)
- Derwent (patents)

Market reports

An increasing number of research companies and report publishers are distributing their product on the Internet. Not only does this make reports more accessible but it can also lower the cost of data. Hard-copy reports are available only as complete works, regardless of the amount of the data within them that are relevant to the user. On-line versions of reports can often be accessed by the page or table at a price set for each data set.

The key publishers to be aware of for competitive intelligence are shown below though the list is far from comprehensive:

- A.C. Nielsen – sales by retail channels
- Datamonitor
- Economist Intelligence Unit
- Espicom (healthcare)
- Euromonitor (consumer products)

- Find/SVP
- Freedonia
- Frost & Sullivan
- Gartner Group (IT businesses)
- Goulden Reports (electrical markets)
- IAL Consultants (chemicals)
- IDC (IT businesses)
- Keynote (consumer products)
- Mintel (consumer products)
- Roskill (minerals)
- Taylor Nelson Sofres (consumer products)

Company news

Company news is provided in the national, local and trade press but is also covered in specialist databases accessible on the web. Most are long-established news providers that have successfully moved into the age of the Internet. A number of them have packaged their data specifically for competitive intelligence, recognising that it is an important new community for them to service.

The main names to look out for are:

- Associated Press
- Reuters
- Dow Jones
- Hoover's Online
- Moody's Investors Services
- Northern Lights
- Standard & Poors
- Kompass
- Thomas Register

Financial data

The web has facilitated the process of obtaining financial data on companies. A number, though far from all, official company registers can be accessed through the web. In addition there are specialists in the collection of company financial information, such as Dun & Bradstreet, that make their data available through the web.

The more interesting sites to commence with are:

- Companies House
- EDGAR Online
- Investext
- Dun & Bradstreet – Financial databases

In addition most of the world's major stock exchanges have their own websites that include news and share data for companies quoted on them. These may be complemented by sites aimed at investors such as MoneyExtra that operate a portal to other sites offering company reports and appraisals.

Company websites

Company websites are the first port of call for all analysts undertaking competitive intelligence. They can contain substantial amounts of information about companies including:

- A company history
- Divisional structure
- Current activities
- Product ranges and product descriptions
- Partners
- Frequently asked questions
- Staff
- 'White papers' on topics related to the business
- News releases
- Head office and manufacturing locations
- Staff requirements

Some companies appear to have lost all of their inhibitions when building their websites. Others have maintained a minimalist approach and reveal just enough to satisfy the needs of the audiences they are pitching their sites at, mainly customers and potential customers.

The main novelty of the web is that considerable amounts of data can be presented without incurring heavy printing costs. It can also be updated quickly and is therefore never out of date for very long. It has not yet replaced traditional forms of communication completely but is becoming a primary method of reaching target audiences to the extent that most companies now expect to find one for a potential supplier and see it as a sign of obscurity if it does not exist.

The prominence of the website as a promotional tool is a boon to competitive intelligence analysts who are spared the drudgery of calling for literature and scouring exhibition stands and distributors for printed material.

Attack sites

A sub-set of the company Internet sites are 'attack' sites on companies that have been established by ex-employees, dissatisfied customers and various pressure groups. The information contained on them is often truly revealing. An 'attack' site on Intel is said to be consulted regularly by staff in order to find out what is really going on inside the company. There are an estimated 5000 corporate attack sites including most of the big names in banking, retailing, food and other consumer products, airlines, telecommunications and automobiles. Many are very specific in the topics they cover and relate to complaints originated by single consumers while others are fed with a variety of information from diverse sources. Yahoo lists 300 attack sites and CompanyEthics.com provides links to sites that have the word 'sucks' in the URL.[2] The data such sites contain have to be treated with caution since their objective is to cause damage as much as to enlighten and they have a tendency to maximise the amount of bad news and exaggerate. Nevertheless, they should be consulted.

Recruitment

The growth of the web as a recruitment medium has two beneficial side effects for competitive intelligence analysts. First, it provides an additional mechanism for that most difficult of tasks, identifying former employees of competitors. Second, it provides an additional method of searching for the recruitment activities of competitors.

Economic and demographic data

Economic, demographic and international trade data for all countries are widely available on the Internet from national and international agency sources. Some are compiled in useful single sources such as the widely respected CIA Yearbook.

Industry statistics

The web is surprising short of useful industry statistics. Despite the massive amounts of statistical data that are collected and published by national governments, international agencies and industry associations, relatively little has gravitated to the web other than as descriptions of reports that can be purchased. This reflects a trend to make statistical services pay for themselves by charging for data.

There are exceptions, such as the US and Canadian governments, who publish a high proportion of the industrial data they collect on the web, but the rest of the world is poorly served. The UK government statistical service sells data on the web but anyone viewing the web as an alternative to a visit to the local reference library for statistical data will be disappointed.

Other government data

International, national and local governments have taken to the Internet on a major scale as a means of publicising their activities and reporting progress. This has resulted in the publication of considerable amounts of intelligence on aspects of companies' activities that previously might not have been identified. Some samples that illustrate the diversity of intelligence that can be collected are as follows:

- Research collaborations between European companies are covered in detail on European Community sites
- Intelligence on environmental compliance by companies is published on a number of state sites in the USA and national government sites in Europe
- Wage rates specific to industry sectors are published by government labour departments
- Listings of companies that have been awarded government contracts are published in Europe and the USA together with details of the contracts

Conferences and trade shows

The web simplifies procedures for identifying forthcoming conferences and trade shows that might be useful for intelligence gathering. It can also be used to access conference papers that have been presented. Sites such as Eventseeker, Eventsource and Trade Show Directory provide industry-wide listings but in addition there are numerous listings of conferences within specific industry sectors. Conference papers can be accessed through databases such as Lexis but may also be published on the web by the individuals that wrote them or the companies or universities that employ them. The Internet has provided an opportunity for 'vanity publishing' that was previously an option only for those with enough money to pay the printing costs.

Short Cuts

There are several sites that provide useful short cuts to business intelligence on the Internet. Some of the more useful are:[3]

- Business Information Sources on the Internet, by the University of Strathclyde
- Internet Business Library
- The Michigan State University Center for Business Education
- Dow Jones Interactive Web Centre

These sites provide lists of business topics and links to Internet sites that cover them.

Discussion Forums

Discussion forums are meeting places in which those interested in the topic covered by the forum can exchange messages and information and access files. Each forum tends to cover a single topic and can include a message section, file libraries and a conference room. Joining a forum provides analysts with the facility to observe what is going on within it, obtain information and ask questions. It therefore represents a convenient method of obtaining primary intelligence. The main danger is that it is difficult to establish the credentials of the people who inhabit discussion forums. Whilst they may be perfectly legitimate they may also be self-proclaimed experts or, even worse, out to cause mischief. A further danger is that enquiries made on discussion forums may also be monitored by the companies being investigated, thereby providing them with the intelligence that an investigation is in progress.

Discussion forms have two components, message sections and conference rooms.

- Message sections – can be used for obtaining answers to questions on any topic from others entering the forum. Since these can be individuals with an interest in the topic, there is a chance of obtaining an informed response. However, the cautionary words above apply
- Conference rooms – as the name suggests, conference rooms provide a facility for on-line conversations with others in the forum. They provide a similar service to the message section but without the wait

The usefulness of discussion forums varies depending on whether one exists for the topic of interest and who can be accessed and their level of knowledge. However, as the number of Internet connections expands, forums provide an interesting alternative to a telephone search for expertise.

Newsgroups (or Bulletin Boards)

Newsgroups provide another method of communicating with special interest groups, of which there are hundreds of thousands already on the net and new ones being added by the minute. Relevant newsgroups can be identified by using a keyword search in the newsreader programme offered by the Internet service provider. Messages or questions can be posted into a relevant newsgroup in the expectation that they will be read by thousands of people worldwide and that potentially valuable responses will be obtained. The responses are 'threaded' in that they contain the original question plus all the responses and comments that have been made together with the signatures of each person providing a contribution. This tends to make the files extremely large but enables the reader to follow the various threads of the discussion that has taken place. Some groups are edited by an individual who chooses to receive all the responses and decide what is added to the file.

As with forums, the usefulness of a newsgroup depends on the calibre of the contributors to it. Questions can attract a high proportion of uninformed and facile comments and need to be filtered carefully.

Monitoring the Internet

Keeping pace with intelligence on the Internet can be just as difficult as keeping pace in printed media. Relying on manual searches and search engines alone is unlikely to produce comprehensive coverage and can be extremely time consuming. Search engines have two further and more serious problems. First, they cannot identify new additions to the web so sequential searches have to be compared with each other manually in order to isolate new items. This can mean comparing thousands of items, a task which is virtually impossible for the average analyst. Second, search engines are weak when it comes to monitoring the daily news media on a timely basis. This is because they index articles only after a six- to twelve-week delay and cannot pick up those articles that the newspapers remove from their sites within that period.

The main methods of avoiding these problems are to use news databases or news feed services. The news databases, such as Dialog, Reuters, Northern Lights and FT.com, archive news items as they are published and offer searchable databases to their clients. Most require an up-front subscription plus a pay-as-you-go fee for each item extracted. News feed services (or electronic news aggregation services) are based on the output of the newswires and other publishers whose output can be captured on the web. They filter company press releases and other news items according to criteria set by clients and deliver them electronically in batches, normally daily. Their main limitation is the restricted number of sources they can cover, typically 200 to 1200 news sources.

Lower cost and more comprehensive alternatives that can also be customised to individual users are the automated web monitoring services, such as CyberAlert[4] and e-watch. Automated web monitoring services use proprietary software to search and filter items on the totality of the visible web and make regular deliveries of intelligence gathered according to complex search definitions. Their search area includes not only publications but also commercial, academic and government sites, user groups, forums and message boards. Unlike manual searches they can also identify new items that have been added since the previous search.

Notes

1. See, for example, Helen Burwell, *Online Competitive Intelligence* (Facts on Demand Press, Tempe, Ariz., 1999).
2. See Amelia Kassel, *Guide to Internet Monitoring and Clipping* (Cyber-Alert White Paper, www.cyberalert.com/whitepaper.html.
3. Helen Burwell, *op. cit.*
4. Amelia Kassel, *op. cit.*

8 Primary Intelligence Collection Techniques

Primary sources of intelligence represent a means of filling the intelligence gaps left when secondary sources have been exhausted. They can provide the most relevant intelligence but are also the most difficult to access. As with secondary sources, there are internal primary sources and external primary sources, both of which should be covered. Most of those who have studied the availability of competitive intelligence have concluded that internal sources can be extremely productive but are rarely exploited fully. Obviously all of the intelligence that is required can in theory be obtained from external sources. The difficulty lies in the fact that they are rarely easy to identify and there are invariably limits to the depth of information they will disclose, particularly those sources that work within the companies being studied.

Internal Primary Sources

The most valuable information can reside in the heads of the company's own staff. Its value derives from the fact that it has been gained by experience, either with the current or previous employers, and that it can cover aspects of competitors that are more anecdotal than the facts and figures available from published sources.

The staff members most widely referred to as sources of competitive intelligence are those who have previously worked for the competition. Though valuable sources, at least in the early months following their defection, they are far from being the only sources that can contribute to the collection of competitive intelligence.

Internal primary sources include all staff who have acquired intelligence on competitors or have access to sources from which it can be obtained. As employees of the organisation that will use the intelligence they stand to gain by providing it. They should be the easiest sources to work with but it has to be admitted that this is not always the case. Information is still considered as conferring power on its holder and there is often a reluctance to part with anything that might be used to advantage.

The information can be categorised as facts, rumours and guesswork and the greatest danger in the use of human intelligence is that the rumours and guesswork are treated as facts.

Who can contribute

Almost anyone that has contact with the outside world is in a position to collect intelligence. The most obvious sources are:

- Staff joining from competitors
- Sales staff
- Members of professional associations
- Delegates to trade and industry associations
- Staff attending conferences and seminars
- Staff attending exhibitions and trade shows

Staff joining from competitors

New recruits who have previously worked for competitors can often provide a particularly interesting perspective on the market. Debriefing recruits about their previous companies is a regular process in many companies but needs to be handled carefully to ensure that no ethical boundaries are crossed. Absorbing the experience and intellectual property that a staff member has acquired from previous employers is a legitimate activity and may be a key reason why a particular individual was recruited. However, it can go too far in that the individual may be expected to provide information which is seriously detrimental to the interests of the previous employer.

The boundary between ethical and unethical information expectations from recruits is easy to see at the extremes but far more difficult to interpret in the grey, middle ground. All employers recognise that past employees will use the knowledge and experience they have gained whilst working with them to further their career prospects with a new employer. They expect the employee to recount information about how things are done by their previous employers, the client base and the qualities of their former colleagues. They do not expect, or find it acceptable for a former employee to take and pass on anything tangible which is not in the public domain such as confidential documents and plans – even those they have compiled themselves. But how do you treat detailed information about impending new product launches, albeit not described in detail or documented? Leaks of such information can be damaging to the past employer but the employee's allegiance is to his or her new employer and, however desirable it may be, it is unrealistic to expect staff to remain completely silent.

In most cases the leakage of information via departing employees has but a transitory effect and is treated as a risk of being in business. Just occasionally it becomes a major issue and this is usually when the amount of damage is judged to be severe and the methods of passing on information can be shown to be illegal. When José Ignacio López left General Motors in 1993 to join Volkswagen and was followed by a group of his former colleagues, they took enough information with them for General Motors to initiate a legal case against Volkswagen. In 1997 the move succeeded when General Motors obtained a $1.1 billion settlement from Volkswagen. The General Motors legal team claimed that General Motors had been 'victimised by international piracy of their intellectual property rights'. They asserted that General Motors had been subject to unfair competition practices when former executives illegally took boxes of trade secrets with them when they left the company and used the Racketeer Influenced Corrupt Organisation (RICO) Act to protect GM's intellectual property rights. In 2000 López was accused of industrial espionage in the United States.

A more subtle form of retribution was exacted by Virgin when a former British Airways senior employee joined them but left within weeks claiming that the job was not what he had been promised. In a letter published in the marketing press Virgin refuted his statement and assured him that the files he had brought over with him from British Airways were being posted back to him!

Sales staff

Sales staff meet regularly with customers and distributors and are occasionally in contact with their opposite numbers from competitors. In business-to-business markets, where customers tend to be reasonably well-informed about their suppliers, exchanges with them can yield substantial amounts of intelligence. In business and consumer markets wholesalers and retailers can be useful intelligence sources that sales representatives can question. In order to maximise the intelligence yield the interrogation of customers and distributors must be correctly structured and the sales representatives must be briefed sufficiently for them to be able to distinguish between facts and information that the customer or distributor would like the sales representatives to believe. Price intelligence is particularly sensitive to distortion by customers and distributors because they may stand to gain by convincing sales representatives that their prices are too high.

Using sales representatives as a source of intelligence is subject to two problems. First, sales representatives are not usually the most objective observers of the competitive situation and are prone to hear what they want to hear rather than what is being said. Good sales representatives should be totally biased in favour of their products and their employers and therefore more likely to recognise the weaknesses in competitors rather than their strengths. Attempts to make sales representatives more objective risks diluting their effectiveness in their sales role and should therefore be treated with extreme care.

The second problem is that any activity that takes time away from the primary task of selling means that the sales task may not be performed effectively. Customers do not give sales representatives unlimited access to their time and questions designed to collect intelligence can make major inroads into selling, especially if the sales representatives think they are James Bond and get over-enthusiastic. Over-inquisitiveness about the competition represents a danger in its own right. Customers can interpret it as a sign of insecurity, which they may then translate into evidence of competitive weakness. Competitive intelligence is valuable but not so much so that it is worth risking sales in order to obtain it.

Sales representatives are best when they obtain intelligence by listening or observing rather than by direct questioning. Unprovoked (or moderately stimulated) comments about competitors by customers or distributors, information obtained from documents seen in customers' premises (often upside down), documents collected from customer reception areas, observed activities, such as deliveries being made by competitors, and industry gossip can be more valuable than direct questioning and intrusive probing.

Members of professional, trade and industry associations

Members of professional associations and delegates to trade and industry bodies have frequent and entirely legitimate opportunities to meet with the staff of competitors. Whilst papers presented at meetings and the subject matter of subsequent discussions may themselves be useful, the real benefit arises from the opportunity to ask the staff of competitors direct questions over coffee or during dinners. Obviously a considerable amount of 'verbal fencing' takes place at such meetings as each delegate attempts to maximise the information they obtain yet minimise what they give away, but as in any encounter there is an almost inevitable flow of intelligence.

Staff attending conferences and seminars

Conferences and seminars provide another opportunity to meet competitors and exchange views. Many delegates find the breaks between sessions infinitely more valuable than the sessions themselves since they provide an informal setting for exchanges.

Staff attending exhibitions and trade shows

Exhibitions and trade shows are mechanisms for disseminating information about exhibitors' products and services and, not surprisingly, they are a happy hunting ground for those seeking intelligence. Their usefulness is enhanced by the fact that they permit contact with competitor staff outside the protection of their offices and in a frame of mind which encourages openness rather than secrecy. The availability of refreshments and alcohol can add to the feeling of goodwill towards visitors to their stands. As public shop windows manned by the suppliers' own staff, exhibitions and trade shows provide a unique opportunity to:

- Examine competitive products
- Identify the product features that are being promoted as unique or new
- Collect brochures, product descriptions and company handouts
- Talk to sales and technical staff
- Hear the current marketing pitch being made

Since exhibitions are usually attended by a number of competitors they are a highly efficient method of collecting intelligence and permit comparisons between competitors.

The use of an exhibition or trade show as a source of intelligence is further enhanced by the fact anybody can attend. A serious data collection exercise will involve multiple attendance by technical and marketing staff each with a different objective.

Motivating staff to participate

To maximise the value of internal intelligence, staff need to be motivated to collect it and provide reports on a regular basis. This is more difficult than it sounds. With a few exceptions, notably the sales force, collecting information is not a natural part of the daily routine of most staff nor are they necessarily in a position to assess the significance of the information they obtain. Nevertheless, a system for information collection and some type of formal or informal encouragement to report intelligence should be put in place to maximise the information flow. The danger in doing so is that the information flow may be overstimulated and that too much useless or inaccurate information will be reported, potentially resulting in a loss of credibility in the system.

The flow of competitive intelligence from internal sources requires:

- Careful briefing of all staff that are in a position to collect intelligence covering the reasons why the intelligence is required, the applications for which it will be used and the types of intelligence that are likely to be of value
- A reporting system that makes it easy for staff to pass on the intelligence they have collected to a central reception point
- A feedback process that provides those that can use intelligence (as well as collect it) with findings that will help them perform better, and those that can only collect intelligence with the reassurance that they are performing a valuable task
- (Potentially) a reward system: they have sometimes been considered but it is extremely difficult to come up with anything that will work on a long-term basis. The best reward is visible evidence that intelligence collected is being used and is useful

The accuracy of internal information

The fact that intelligence is available from internal sources does not mean that it is necessarily accurate. Sales people are not the only staff members that can lose their objectivity when observing competitors. Folklore and wishful thinking are just as likely to be believed as hard facts by all staff, especially if they show the competitors in a bad light. It is therefore essential to verify all internal intelligence. Some of the key checks are:

- The time intelligence was obtained – old intelligence is likely to be less accurate or representative of the current situation than recent information
- The method by which the intelligence was acquired – intelligence that has been collected from first-hand sources (for example, from customers or competitors' staff) may be more reliable than indirect reports
- Who acquired the intelligence – some internal sources are more objective and reliable than others and some are in a better position to establish the accuracy (or inaccuracy) of intelligence
- The purpose for which the data were acquired – data may be biased or incomplete because they were obtained to solve a highly specific problem

External Primary Intelligence

When secondary and internal sources of intelligence have been exhausted the competitive intelligence professional turns to primary intelligence gathering from external sources. It is last in the list for very good reasons. It is technically the most challenging, can be carried out only by the most skilled researchers and is by far the most costly method of collecting intelligence. Furthermore, nobody who abides by the ethical constraints of the competitive intelligence community can guarantee success. There are too many factors that can frustrate the effectiveness of the primary intelligence collection process, not the least of which is a flat refusal of respondents to cooperate when the questioning gets too sensitive.

Sources of external primary intelligence

Primary intelligence collection from external sources relies on two conditions:

- That fragments of information collected from diverse sources can be pieced together to reveal enough of the overall picture and some of the detail
- That there are numerous people in a variety of organisations who are in a position to provide a complete or partial view on competitors' activities

Competitive intelligence can be likened to building jigsaw puzzles of a landscape when significant proportions of the pieces are missing. The overall content of the picture is likely to be revealed, some of the detail will be present and other details will be missing but can possibly be guessed. The problem of determining what is there will depend not only on the proportion of the total pieces that are collected but also how they are spread over the complete canvas. The problem of interpretation becomes really serious only when every piece collected is blue and none of them has a straight edge!

The key to success lies in the diversity of sources that can be identified and accessed. Any intelligence-gathering activity that relies on a few contacts has only a limited chance of success. As the number of potential sources that can be tapped expands, the chances of finding any specific item of intelligence increase dramatically. Fortunately in all markets there are a large number of individuals who may know what is going on. They include:

- Subject company staff
- Ex-employees now working in other companies
- The staff of other competitors
- Customers
- Suppliers
- Brokers' analysts
- Journalists
- The staff of regulatory authorities
- Professional and trade association staff
- Industry research organisations
- Pressure groups
- Universities and business schools
- Consultants
- Chambers of Commerce

The staff of the competitors being studied

The most accurate sources of intelligence are staff working within the companies being studied. By all normal standards they should also be the least likely people to be willing to engage in a dialogue. A common comment that is made when discussing competitive intelligence is, 'if anyone asked me questions like that, there is no way I would answer them'. If this were true for everybody competitive intelligence would be extremely difficult and unproductive but the fact is that employees do reveal information. They do so when they:

- Do not feel that the information they are being asked for is confidential
- Are engaged in a dialogue from which they feel they stand to benefit by learning something

- Feel they are in control of the discussion and will reveal only the information they are prepared to release
- Are not suspicious about the reason for the discussion
- Are asked for information which it is their job to provide
- Have no inhibitions about revealing information

This usually means that the competitor staff who are most likely to cooperate are the most senior and the most junior. Middle management are more inclined to be nervous and aware of the real or imaginary dangers to their job security if they make an error and release too much information. Senior management normally have the confidence to feel they can control the situation; junior staff are less likely to be aware of the risks, but they may also be less knowledgeable.

The staff to approach depends entirely on the types of information required but the most productive sources of intelligence tend to be:

- Product and brand managers
- Staff with a responsibility for advertising or below-the-line activities
- Sales representatives and sales engineers
- Service engineers
- Call centre staff
- Production management
- Product design staff
- Staff with the responsibility for investor relations
- Information officers
- Market research personnel

The staff to avoid are accountants, human resources managers and competitive intelligence staff.

Ex-employees

Ex-employees suffer from fewer inhibitions than current employees and, provided they can be located within a reasonable time after leaving the company, they can be valuable sources. The key problem is locating them. In most circumstances they are few in number and although a high proportion tend to stay within the same industry sector, there are very few guides to where they may be. Even the growing number of CVs posted to recruitment websites are a drop in the ocean compared to the total level of employment, and locating a knowledgeable ex-employee by that route within the timeframe for the analysis is likely to be a lucky rather than a planned event. The planned identification of ex-employees requires a careful trawl of knowledgeable sources within and outside competitors. Potential contacts in this context include:

- Former colleagues (where did they go?), though this assumes that it is known that a particular staff member has left
- New colleagues
- Recruitment consultancies specialising in the sector

Other competitors

Although most respondents can be expected to be reluctant to discuss the activities of their own companies, they are usually less inhibited about discussing other competitors. This is especially true if they feel they can learn something. The most common difficulty is that central sources may be equally unaware of other competitors' activities and if they are knowledgeable they may have paid a substantial amount for the data and are unlikely to give them away freely. Nevertheless, the outward-facing staff of all participants in a market can be expected to have obtained intelligence in the course of their day-to-day activities and they also include staff who have worked previously for the companies being targeted. It is therefore logical to use them as an extended contact base for competitor intelligence.

Customers

In business markets customers have access to considerable amounts of information on their suppliers. This is imparted not only during the selling process but also during the casual exchanges that take place when supplier and customer meet. Unlocking this source can provide a powerful injection of factual intelligence, rumour and gossip, though customers are generally reluctant to provide intelligence that they think might harm their own interests or their relationship with important suppliers.

For companies collecting intelligence on their own behalf, customers fall into three categories: customers they currently supply, customers they have supplied in the past and potential customers. Contact with current customers can be regular and sufficiently friendly to expect some level of exchange of intelligence about the activities of other suppliers. Relationships with potential customers are likely to be less cordial and, although a flow of intelligence can be stimulated, care must be taken to avoid creating a situation that could threaten a sale. Relationships with ex-customers may still be friendly and there is less to lose by quizzing them.

Competitive intelligence consultants collecting intelligence on be-half of clients have neither the advantages of friendly relationships with customers nor the problems of projecting the wrong image. For them customers represent a large community of intelligence sources that can be trawled for as long as time and budget permit.

Suppliers

Like customers, suppliers into competitor companies also have access to intelligence, which, depending on the nature of their contractual relationship, it may be possible to access. The existence of non-disclosure agreements may prevent them from participating in an intelligence-gathering exercise, but these tend to apply only when the supplier had to be given extremely sensitive information in order to provide the service required or to manufacture the product being supplied.

Most companies have a wide range of suppliers and the nature and volume of what is purchased from them can provide considerable insight into their activities. The spectrum of purchases includes:

- Raw materials
- Components and sub-assemblies
- Production equipment
- Consumables
- Packaging
- Logistics and delivery services
- Stationery
- Printing services

Competitive intelligence literature abounds with descriptions of how packaging suppliers have provided vital clues on production volumes, how delivery schedules have enabled customer bases to be traced or how information obtained from brochure printers has provided evidence of a planned new product launch or a price rise. In reality direct evidence of competitors' activities of this type is extremely difficult to obtain and suppliers are more generally useful as sources of the rumour and gossip that may also be obtained from customers.

Brokers' analysts

All quoted companies are reported on regularly by stockbrokers. The official broker for a company has a responsibility to promote its clients' shares as well as undertake the various tasks required by the Stock Exchange; other brokers study companies to provide investment advice to their share-buying clients. Quoted companies provide considerable amounts of information to the analysts working in brokers in order to enable them to make accurate assessments of future performance. Misleading the investment community is not something that is encouraged, though when the news is bad companies may be defensive and less informative. Although brokers' analysts rely heavily on companies for their information and have full access to investor relations staff to get it, they still endeavour to extend their knowledge and verify the facts they have been given by carrying out independent research of their own. It is at this point that the competitive intelligence analyst and the broker's analyst come together with a mutual interest.

Identifying the brokers that follow the companies being studied and establishing contact with them should be one of the first steps in an intelligence programme covering public companies. To be made productive analysts need to be fed and it is therefore helpful to have data that can be traded with them. It is also useful to identify topics that the analysts are interested in – usually those that companies are reluctant to cover themselves. These can be included in the scope of the project for the specific purpose of rewarding analysts, even if they are not required for the client.

Journalists

Journalists that report on business and companies are in a similar position to the brokers' analysts and are afforded similar contact privileges. Knowledgeable journalists can be found working for the national press, the local press, the relevant trade press and as freelancers.

The interests of journalists are not restricted to quoted companies or even large companies. The local press can cover small companies that are important or newsworthy in their local community. They may also report on the activities of divisions of large companies that can be invisible at a national level. Trade press journalists can get closer to their subjects partly because they have a continuing interest and partly because they have specialised industry knowledge.

Journalists make their living out of information and are generally willing to discuss the activities of a company they have covered providing there is a chance they will learn something in the process. As with the brokers it is therefore helpful to have information to trade when approaching them.

The most common tactic in competitive intelligence is to identify journalists that have filed a story on a company being investigated and interview them for any background not contained in the published item. It is not always the case that additional information exists since news items are often based exclusively on press releases by the companies themselves. The best items to follow up on are those that contain an investigative component and where the journalist has made an obvious attempt to get behind the official story.

When interviewing journalists it is useful to remember that journalists working to tight deadlines do not always have time to verify the facts they report and that once a story has been filed their interest often ceases.

Regulatory authority staff

In regulated industries the staff of the regulatory bodies have close and constant contact with the companies whose activities they regulate. They may be reluctant to discuss the activities of specific companies in detail but they may be prepared to provide background to any reports that they issue.

Professional and trade association staff

The staff of professional and trade associations are close to their members, particularly those that are most active in the association, and are likely to have informed opinions as well as access to facts. Other members of the association can access these most easily. Outsiders have difficulties that arise from the fact that associations tend to work on the wholly reasonable assumption that they are in existence to help the members that pay their subscriptions rather than non-members.

Industry research organisations

In many manufacturing industries research associations have been established to carry out technical research on behalf of members. Although the decline in manufacturing industry has meant that a number of these have been disbanded or passed into private ownership, many still survive in their original form. They are staffed by technical experts who have wide contacts within the industries they service and who are potentially knowledgeable on developments by member companies.

Pressure groups

Pressure groups embrace a diversity of subjects, many of which cover commercial activity. Whether for or against an activity they amass all types of information about governments and companies that they feel will help their cause. Their willingness to disclose intelligence on companies may depend on whether they feel that by doing so they will obtain new information or help their cause. They may also suffer from a biased view of the world and any data they provide will require careful corroboration before they are accepted as accurate.

Universities and business schools

Experts on a number of industries can be found in specialist departments within universities and business schools. They devote considerable time to tracking developments and following the activities of companies and are normally very willing to participate in discussions.

Consultants

Consultants specialising in industry sectors collect large amounts of intelligence in order to support their consulting activity or provide a basis for reports that they publish. They are generally unwilling to provide intelligence unless they are paid for it but an exchange of information may be possible if they feel that the researcher has access to sources or intelligence that they have not managed to obtain themselves.

Chambers of Commerce

Local Chambers of Commerce act as a voice for member companies in the localities in which they are based. In some countries membership is mandatory but in most it is optional. The staff of Chambers of Commerce are not likely to reveal detailed intelligence on their members but they can be extremely useful on such topics as trading and employment conditions in the region, taxation and local regulations affecting business.

Obtaining Intelligence Directly from Competitors

Companies seeking intelligence directly from their competitors have two options: use their own staff to collect it or use an external intelligence collection agency. Using staff to collect intelligence suffers from one serious disadvantage – the competitors normally know who they are and therefore why they are interested. Although some activities can be carried out incognito, such as examining competitors' products on exhibition stands, any form of direct questioning will provoke those on the receiving end to ask for the identity of the questioner and why they are interested. Unless staff are prepared to lie (not a practice to be considered under any circumstances) the shutters will inevitably come down.

This does not mean that direct questioning by staff is impossible, only that the results may be limited in value. Intelligence that is shared between competitors, particularly in situations where they could be accused under antitrust legislation, tends to be little more than each party would be happy to publish. It is therefore more common to use external consultants for the task. Fortunately there are a number of consultancies that specialise in the provision of intelligence-gathering services for clients. These have developed skills that maximise their chances of obtaining what is required but above all else they shield the identity of their clients. An open display of interest in a competitor is, in itself, intelligence that is best kept secret.

Questioning competitor staff

Whoever carries out the task, covert questioning of the staff of competitors is the very apex of the range of competitive intelligence skills. It is the equivalent of entering the lion's den and carries with it not only the risk of failure but also the risk of exposure. The worst outcome of a failed primary intelligence-gathering exercise would be one in which no intelligence is obtained, the target company finds out that an intelligence operation against them is in progress, identifies the means by which the intelligence is being sought and identifies the competitor seeking it. This would provide the target company with an intelligence coup, permitting them to scream 'foul' to the rest of the world and then take steps to frustrate any further attempts.

The difficulties involved in questioning the staff of competitors means that careful consideration must be given to whether it should be attempted and, if so, how it should be done.

When deciding whether interrogating competitors is worthwhile there are a few simple questions that can be asked:

- What value is ascribed to the intelligence if it is collected?
- Is the collection programme likely to succeed?
- Even if the programme succeeds what are the chances of being caught?
- If the programme is discovered, how serious are the likely consequences in terms of exposure and adverse publicity?

High risks of failure, being caught and exposure may be worthwhile if the value of the intelligence is extremely high, but not otherwise. Those planning the programme should be asked to assign a probability to the likelihood of them being able to deliver the intelligence. If it is between 50 per cent and 80 per cent the exercise is probably worth trying. If it is 90–100 per cent they are either over-optimistic or have some reason to know that the intelligence is available.

Maximising the chances of success in primary intelligence collection is not a matter of luck but of careful planning. The main factors to be considered when planning an intelligence-gathering programme involving direct questioning of competitor staff, are:

- Identifying sources
- Initiating the discussion
- Inducements
- The discussion guide
- Relationships

Identifying sources

It is axiomatic that the quality of the sources is the key to the quality of the intelligence. It is therefore imperative that time is spent identifying sources and verifying their credentials to provide the information requested. The options for identifying individual sources are:

- Secondary research
  - Papers and presentations
  - Company websites
  - Recruitment sites
  - Appointment announcements
- Switchboard
- The reference trail

Secondary research.   Secondary research can be used to identify staff members who have written papers or spoken at conferences. Staff thus identified are easy to approach since their papers or presentations can be used to initiate a conversation. Company websites may list staff members together with their area of responsibility but a visit to the rapidly growing number of recruitment websites may also identify individuals working in specific companies. Announcements of new appointments in the national, professional, trade or local press can be equally productive.

Switchboards. Getting through to staff through the switchboard by job function rather than by name is becoming increasingly difficult as companies seek to protect themselves from the ravages of head-hunters or improve efficiency by cutting out telephone operators. It is therefore advisable to spend some time trying to identify named individuals to approach using the methods identified above. This is less difficult when tracking an industry on a continuous basis since, over time, it is possible to construct a network of contacts.

Where direct-dialling systems are in use, an alternative to using the operator is to dial numbers using the area code prefix and the first two digits of the switchboard number followed by a random final two digits. In most cases this will route to a staff member who can then be used as a source for the correct contact. On some switchboards a redirected call from another internal number has a different ring tone and may therefore bypass the screening practice applied to external calls.

The reference trail. Once one contact has been identified he or she should be used as a source of additional contacts within their own and other companies. The ability to refer to a previous source has some effect in reducing suspicion, especially if they know them well.

Initiating a dialogue

The most difficult task when questioning the staff of competitors is initiating the dialogue. The effectiveness of a discussion with a potential source is determined in the first few minutes (some would say seconds!) of the conversation after contact has been made. It is at this stage that the respondent is most suspicious and least inclined to cooperate. As the conversation proceeds barriers tend to be lowered and the information flow increases.

One of the most common questions from respondents when first approached is 'How did you get my name?' Respondents need to be reassured that the process is legitimate and they are not the targets of a plot. Being able to say 'I have been given your name by Mr X who thought that you might be able to help me' is a more reassuring response to the question than 'I was put through to you by the switchboard'. Ideally Mr X would be their boss or a respected colleague, but this is too much to hope for; it is equally possible that Mr X would prove to be someone they have no respect for. A useful additional method of lowering the defences is to state that the respondent has been identified as an 'expert' in that field. Being accorded guru status is not only flattering but also increases willingness to provide the facts and opinions that usually emanate from gurus!

Unfortunately it is necessary to cover the two most difficult topics in an intelligence-gathering exercise at the beginning of a conversation. These are the identity of the organisation that requires the information and what it is required for. If a direct and honest answer is given to both of these questions it is virtually certain that no intelligence will be obtained. The exceptions are those rare contacts that display no curiosity and are happy to talk.

So what should be said? The Code of Ethics under which competitive intelligence is collected specifies no lying, no misrepresentation, no law-breaking and no bribery. Fortunately they do not stipulate that the complete truth is told. This means that:

- A consultant can identify his own employing company (that is, the consultancy) without revealing the name of the sponsor of the analysis
- In response to a direct question, a consultant can state that the sponsor has asked to remain anonymous
- It is fair and truthful to state that an analysis is being undertaken of an industry or market and those companies that are operating within it, without elaborating by stating specifically that it is a competitive intelligence programme
- It is acceptable to induce cooperation by engaging the respondent's interest or curiosity and the promise that they will learn something from the exchange
- It is acceptable to use intelligence already gathered as a bargaining chip or as a stimulus to initiate a discussion

Inducements

The main inducement to cooperate is the promise that the conversation will be worthwhile to both parties. The offer to trade or pool information has a far better chance of success than a request for information to be provided.

There are many situations in which useful exchanges of information can take place between the staff of competitive companies, especially when they know each other and there is strong mutual advantage in sharing knowledge. It can happen when both companies:

- Face a common external threat that can be dealt with more effectively by pooling their intelligence
- Stand to make efficiency gains by pooling information on their business processes

- Can solve joint problems, such as recruitment or training, more effectively by sharing information
- Can extend their knowledge on third parties by pooling their intelligence

Consultants are more likely to use the intelligence they have already collected in their programmes as means of inducing cooperation from future respondents. Obviously they cannot do this to the extent that they give away everything that their client has paid for, but on the basis that it is always difficult to 'get without giving', it is legitimate to pass on some intelligence either as a primer for the discussion or as recompense.

Discussion guide

No discussion with competitors' staff should be carried out without a guide that sets out the planned progress of the discussion. The basic rules of discussion guide construction are:

- Whatever is really intended or even proves to be practical, present the discussion as an exchange and avoid the suggestion that the information flow will be all one-way
- Never plan to overload a respondent with topics. Many analysts try to obtain a wide range of intelligence from a single respondent on the basis that he or she may prove to be the only person who will speak to them. Whilst this expectation may be fulfilled, it is better to plan for a shorter first discussion and come back for more at a later date than to attempt to get all that is needed in one session
- Prioritise the intelligence into 'must ask', 'try to ask' and 'ask if all is going well' categories. This will help ensure that the essential topics are covered in the event of an early shut-down of the discussion
- Within each group, the topics should be sequenced so that they commence with the least sensitive and move on to the most sensitive. Respondents are at their most cautious and most nervous at the beginning of the discussion. As time progresses they generally become more confident and more willing to cooperate
- Ensure that the questions are tailored to the probable knowledge of each respondent and that no one is asked questions that they cannot conceivably answer. Repeated admissions of ignorance can induce an early termination of the discussion
- Despite the point above, always bear in mind that some staff may have knowledge outside their normal sphere of operations and, unaware of its significance, be less reluctant to reveal it
- Ask direct questions as infrequently as possible. Use the information already obtained to lead the discussion. It is far better to ask

respondents for clarification or to confirm or deny what has been picked up from other sources than to ask direct questions
- Remember that when it comes to numerical information, asking for brackets and approximations is more likely to produce a response than a request for precise data
- Ensure that as many as possible of the awkward situations that can arise in the discussion are anticipated in advance and that responses have already been framed. These will include repeated requests for the identity of the sponsor and requests for access to the final results

The term 'discussion guide' has been used deliberately. Unlike market research, competitive intelligence should never use questionnaires. These may be comprehensive and structured but they are also rigid. In intelligence gathering the analyst must be free to respond to any statements made by respondents that appear to provide an opportunity for interesting supplementary questions. The more the discussion appears to flow as a conversation and the less it seems like an interrogation, the greater the chances of success.

Relationships

When intelligence is sought regularly in the same industry sector it is possible to build a network of contacts amongst competitors for the purpose of exchanging information on best practices. All parties must be prepared to give something but stand to gain much in return. When this happens care must be taken to ensure that any exchanges that could be construed as 'collusion', especially discussions on prices, are avoided.

Naive or knowledgeable

When questioning respondents, analysts have the option of being naive on the subject matter or knowledgeable. Naivety offers the prospect that respondents will not perceive a threat and will explain matters fully. The main risk is that respondents will think the enquiry is frivolous and will refuse to cooperate. Being knowledgeable suggests that the enquirer is worth dealing with and may provide some valuable information. Being too knowledgeable may raise suspicions. The balance is difficult to achieve and the effectiveness of either approach will vary from respondent to respondent. It is commonly the case that female researchers working in male environments, such as engineering or chemicals will benefit from a naive approach. Whether the same is true of male researchers working in female environments, such as cosmetics, remains to be proved.

Graphology

Although graphology was long regarded as one of the blacker arts as far as business applications were concerned, it is now widely accepted, especially in continental European countries, that the analysis of handwriting provides a valuable guide to personality. As such it has gained widespread use in the screening of job applicants. Although rarely used on its own in the selection of candidates it can show personality traits that are difficult to uncover by conventional interviews. It is therefore logical that in order to understand the personality and skills of the executives and key staff of competitor companies an analysis of their handwriting should be carried out. One of the key advantages of handwriting analysis is that it covers the totality of the writer's personality and can cover attributes such as leadership, energy, drive, enthusiasm, organisational ability and sociability. It can also uncover physical and mental ill health, tendencies to over-indulge in drink or drugs, feelings of resentment, greed and repressions. Obtaining samples of current handwriting may prove problematical but not impossible and the added dimension it can provide to personal profiling makes it well worth the effort.

Reverse engineering

Reverse engineering is a well-established approach to obtaining product intelligence. It involves dismantling competitors' products in order to learn their features, the materials that have been used, how they are constructed, the design of components, finishing and the assembly method.

Overcoming the roadblocks

When gathering primary intelligence it is normal to encounter a number of roadblocks. These work in addition to suspicions of the motives for enquiries referred to above. Overcoming the roadblocks calls for high levels of ingenuity and even then they may prove insurmountable. The most common barriers are:

- Switchboards
- Voicemail
- Lack of availability or time to cooperate
- E-mail
- Counter-intelligence

Switchboards

Getting through to staff through the switchboard by job function rather than by name is becoming increasingly difficult as companies seek to protect themselves from the ravages of head-hunters or improve efficiency by cutting out telephone operators. It is therefore advisable to spend some time trying to identify named individuals to approach using the methods identified above. This is less difficult when tracking an industry on a continuous basis since, over time, it is possible to construct a network of contacts.

Where direct-dialling systems are in use, an alternative to using the operator is to dial numbers using the area code prefix and the first two digits of the switchboard number followed by a random final two digits. In most cases this will route to a staff member who can then be used as a source for the correct contact. On some switchboards a redirected call from another internal number has a different ring tone and may therefore bypass the screening practice applied to external calls.

Voicemail

One of the main barriers to initiating a discussion is the increasing use of voicemail. Meant as a method of receiving messages whilst absent from an office, voicemail seems to be growing in use as a method of screening calls. Messages left on voicemail are rarely responded to unless the caller or the company they are calling from is known or there is some inducement to respond. Calls from telesales and market and other research organisations are widely ignored. There are few methods of dealing with voicemail except persistence.

A more controllable method of stimulating a response is through the message that is left. A combination of an interesting 'voice' and a tantalising message may provoke sufficient interest to achieve a call back. However, this is not a route down which analysts should progress too far. Messages that are highly provoking may result in so much disappointment when the call back is made that the respondent refuses to cooperate further.

Lack of availability or time to cooperate

An inability to make contact with key respondents either because they are physically absent from their offices or unable to spare the time to respond to questions is a common roadblock. The only workable response to this problem is to allow sufficient time for them to become available. If this cannot be achieved within the time frame for the survey alternative respondents should be sought. Theoretically they could be tracked down to their homes or to the locations in which they are working or called on their mobiles. Unless it is known that the respondents are prepared to accept calls away from their offices, the risk in all three approaches is that the analyst may antagonise the respondent to the point that they will refuse to cooperate.

E-mail

The third most common roadblock is a request for an e-mail (or fax) setting out the purpose of the enquiry and the topics that will be covered in the discussion. Often this information is sought in the hope that the enquirer will not make further enquiries. Unfortunately this may well be the case since written notification not only makes the nature of the enquiry explicit, it also gives the respondent time to reflect. Complying with a request for a written explanation is worth doing only when the nature of the enquiry can be made to sound compelling and innocent.

Counter-intelligence

The existence of a counter-intelligence programme can cause a complete shut-down to enquiries and, if well executed, can be extremely difficult to circumvent within the target organisation. Normally the best method of evading its effect is to concentrate the search on external sources of intelligence.

The Demise of Primary Intelligence?

Direct interrogation of competitors has never been easy and can only increase in difficulty as awareness of competitive intelligence spreads. The use of intelligence by companies heightens their sensitivity to intelligence programmes carried out against them. The introduction of counter-intelligence programmes will have the same effect. The response to any erosion of the ability to collect direct intelligence can only be greater inventiveness in both the collection and interpretation of information. With fewer pieces of the jigsaw available it will be more difficult to deduce the full picture unless more effective inter-pretation techniques are deployed.

9 Market Research as a Source of Competitive Intelligence

Market researchers often seek to distance themselves from competitive intelligence, usually on the grounds that the provision of such information infringes their code of practice. In doing so they ignore the fact that some of the most valuable information about competitors is provided by standard market research techniques and programmes. Indeed it is difficult to see how a market can be fully analysed without taking account of the competitive environment and many of today's most effective competitive intelligence analysts cut their teeth in the market research business rather than starting out in the intelligence world.

Although there are significant differences between market research and competitive intelligence the two disciplines have more in common than market researchers tend to think. Many of the customer analysis services that have been designed to help marketing staff to format their own marketing programmes can also be applied to the study of competitors' clients.

Market Research and Competitive Intelligence

Market research is widely associated with the analysis of customers. Whilst it is true that customer surveys form a major part of the market research business, customers are not the only targets for analysis. Market researchers spend considerable time studying retail and wholesale distributors, service providers such as transport and logistics companies, professionals, advisers, specifiers such as architects and opinion leaders such as politicians and journalists. Indeed any type of individual and organisation that plays a role in a market can be included in the scope of a market research survey. Competitive intelligence does the same. It uses all sources that have knowledge of the activities of suppliers (competitors) in a market, including customers, to build its intelligence base. The data-gathering techniques used in competitive intelligence are broadly similar to those used in market research, though the mechanics by which they are applied are quite different, as is the interpretation of the results.

The key difference between market research and competitive intelligence is in the primary focus of the information that is gathered. Whereas market research is largely concerned with the collective requirements, activities and behaviour of the customer groups that make up a market, competitive intelligence is concerned exclusively with the activities of suppliers into a market, their performance and their plans. Market research does not normally report on the activities of individual customers but competitive intelligence does provide information on each competitor.

Customers as a Source of Intelligence

The common ground that market researchers and competitive intelligence analysts often overlook is the use of customers as a source of intelligence. In consumer markets customers can provide data on their perceptions, their use and their preferences with respect to competitive suppliers of all the products they purchase. These data are collected regularly by consumer product manufacturers for marketing purposes but not always seen as being part of the competitive intelligence process. In industrial markets use and perceptual data on suppliers can also be collected but in many cases the customer is also a potential source of direct intelligence on competitors' activities. The exchange of information between suppliers and buyers of industrial products is significantly higher than that which is required in consumer marketing and increases as the value of the purchase goes up. Buyers committing multi-million pound sums to the acquisition of raw materials, equipment or key services need considerable reassurance that the supplier is reputable and is likely to stay in business long enough not only to fulfil the contract but also to provide long-term support. This means that they develop a relationship with suppliers that results in a high level of knowledge of their suppliers' activities. Tapping into this knowledge is part of the skills developed by competitive intelligence analysts.

Surveying Markets for Intelligence

The range of market research services that can be used to provide competitive intelligence is surprisingly wide and none of them require any modification to make them useful. The data that can be obtained are both quantitative and qualitative. The quantitative data permit analysts to position competitors within the markets they are servicing with a considerable degree of precision. The qualitative data permit analysts to understand how the competitors are perceived at the sharp end of the competitive battle, namely by their customers. Using qualitative research it is possible to detect impending problems for competitors some time before they are reflected in performance.

The following sections describe the market research services that can be used for competitive intelligence and the types of data they can generate.

Panels and retail audits

Consumer panels, retail audits and specialist audits, such as hospital panels, supply data that are heavily competitor-orientated. Although users of panel data may see them primarily as a method of tracking their own performance their real usefulness arises when they are used to track the performance of competitors. The data that can be obtained from panels and retail audits include:

- Total sales within a product category
- Sales by distribution channel
- Regional sales
- Sales by customer category
- Brand (or supplier) shares
- Brand shares per distribution channel
- Brand shares within each region
- Brand preferences of each customer category
- Prices paid per brand in each distribution channel and region
- Growth in total sales
- Growth in brand sales and market share changes

The ability to commission special analysis of the panel data means that it is possible to access additional intelligence such as the launch and success of promotional initiatives by competitors. Indeed the availability of panel-generated competitor data to suppliers of consumer goods eliminates the need for direct interrogation of competitors on any subjects relating to sales and the segments of the market they are servicing.

Awareness surveys

Awareness surveys are a standard market research process for measuring the degree of exposure suppliers have succeeded in achieving in a market. Customers tend to purchase from suppliers that they have heard of and feel they can trust. High levels of unaided recall and the creation of a favourable impression of the company are therefore key objectives of most marketing and promotional programmes.

In awareness surveys it is normal to measure the awareness of competitors as well as that of the research sponsor. If a company is to maximise its impact in a marketplace, awareness levels need to be not only high but also as high as, or even higher than, those of competitors. Competitors' awareness profiles tell much about the intensity of their promotional effort and the success they have achieved. Before attempting to emulate a clever marketing initiative by a competitor it is worth checking its effectiveness in terms of the awareness level it has actually achieved.

Image surveys

It is said that 'a pound of image is worth a ton of performance' and nowhere is this statement truer than in marketing. Competitors abound that have images that are far worse or far better than their actual performance would seem to justify. Corporate images are based on a large number of factors not all of which are controllable by the current management of the companies themselves. Historical performance can be more influential than current performance. Memories of bad performance linger long after the problems that created it have been cured. The privatisation of state-owned companies did not change their reputation for being bureaucratic overnight. The country of origin can have a beneficial or an adverse effect that outweighs the quality of the service or product provided, as McDonald's has found to its advantage in Russia and to its cost in France.

It is also said that 'perception is reality' and however much a company may disagree with the judgement of customers the image that customers retain of suppliers is a powerful contributor to their performance. This means that if the image projected by competitors is known it will provide a guide to the success they are likely to enjoy when promoting their services. It may also explain why some competitors' marketing budgets work more effectively than others. Competitors with a poor image have to spend proportionately more to achieve the same effect as those with a favourable image.

Customer satisfaction surveys

Customer satisfaction surveys measure the extent to which companies meet the expectations of their customers. This complements image profiling by covering the tangible aspects of performance. The measurements usually involve identifying the product and service criteria that customers consider when evaluating supplier performance and then obtaining customer ratings of performance on each criterion. High average ratings on criteria that are also regarded as being extremely important indicate supplier strengths whereas low weightings on high-importance criteria indicate problems.

The criteria normally include those that relate directly to the product or service supplied, such as its quality, consistency or performance, and those that relate to the service support that is provided, such as delivery speed, delivery reliability, the quality of the suppliers' sales and technical staff, product literature and the clarity and accuracy of billing. Most surveys measure performance on 20–25 evaluation criteria which permits a very detailed examination of performance.

In the past suppliers tended to concentrate on measuring their own performance within their customer base. It is now normal to measure the performance of competitors within their customer bases in order to determine whether a supplier is doing better or worse than the competition. The same results provides a clear indication of the strengths and weaknesses of competitors and, with repetitive measurements over time, can show which aspects of their product and service package they are investing in.

Loyalty surveys

Loyalty surveys use relatively simple questions to test whether customers are likely to remain loyal to their existing suppliers. If applied to competitors, loyalty surveys show the extent to which they have been able to create loyal customer bases and their vulnerability to competitive attack.

Mystery shopping

Mystery shopping is a technique designed to test the sales performance of a supplier. It can be used to report on the effectiveness of sales staff and the extent to which they conform to company procedures. Studies are normally commissioned by companies to test their own selling systems particularly at retail level, but it is obviously tempting to use them as a vehicle to test competitors' performance or even to obtain details of competitors' offers. Pretending to be a customer breaks one of the basic rules of competitive intelligence in that it is clearly misrepresentation. However, it is possible to conceive a survey in which the experience of genuine customers shopping for products or services is captured for competitive intelligence purposes.

Media research

Media research covers a range of services that are designed to test the use and effectiveness of various marketing media. The main types of media research that have a direct application in competitive intelligence are:

- Expenditure by competitors on advertising
- Breakdown of advertising expenditure by type of media
- Analysis of the content of advertising
- Analysis of the effectiveness of competitors' advertising

Perceptual mapping

As the name implies, perceptual mapping provides a picture or a map of a marketplace that defines the perceptions respondents have of products, brands, services or companies. The technique defines the key characteristics by which products, brands and companies could be described and locates the products or brands on these dimensions in accordance with respondents' perceptions. The technique shows the perceived differences between brands or suppliers. Minimal differences, which show up as brands or suppliers mapped in close proximity, indicate strong competition; large differences, which show up as brands or companies in isolation on the map, indicate uniqueness in the marketplace. The results need to be combined with market structure data in order to show whether the territory that the brands or suppliers are perceived as occupying is that in which the supplier actually wishes to be.

For competitive analysis perceptual maps are useful in the analysis of:

- Competitors' product positioning
- Segments serviced by competitors
- Competitors' strengths and weaknesses

10 Analysis – Filling the Gaps and Stretching the Data

Unlike market research, the analytical process in competitive intelligence is not something that begins once data collection has ceased. To obtain the best intelligence, analysis and data collection should run hand in hand until a satisfactory result has been achieved or until it is evident that no further progress can be made. Competitive intelligence analysis is used for two purposes:

- Filling gaps in the data yielded by an intelligence-gathering programme
- Drawing conclusions from the data that extend the understanding of competitors' actions and plans

The combined assaults of secondary and primary intelligence gathering rarely provide detailed responses to all of the intelligence topics. They may cover 80–90 per cent of requirements but there are always items that cannot be covered. These are often the most sensitive issues and therefore the most interesting. By analysing in tandem with data collection it is possible to identify barriers as they arise and to evaluate their implications. It is then possible to develop new lines of questioning and to identify alternative sources of intelligence that may circumvent the barriers.

Once intelligence has been collected analytical techniques can be used to extend the coverage into those aspects of competitors' activities on which it is unreasonable to expect direct evidence to be available. At this point analyses of the company's history, personal profiling and scenario development take over as tools by which a company's probable objectives and the means by which they will seek to achieve them can be deduced. Most of the time spent on competitor analysis is used to obtain data; analytical techniques can convert the data into a deeper understanding of the threat that competitors represent. The data will show what competitors are doing whereas the analysis may reveal why they are doing it.

The labyrinthine twists and turns of a typical investigation in which analysis and interviewing are combined to produce a result are illustrated in the following example. In a survey designed to evaluate a small rubber products company as a potential acquisition candidate it was decided that there were three main sources of intelligence that could be used. The first was the company itself, the second was the customer base and the third was published sources. The company had three lines of business, all of which involved the supply of customised products produced to order for individual clients; it had no standard products. The three lines of business were rubber linings for containers, bridge bearings and rubber-to-metal components for the engineering industry. In the first days of the investigation it was found that the linings business was for a single customer and was relatively straightforward to understand. The two other businesses serviced highly fragmented customer bases and the visibility of the target company was extremely low, mainly because it was a small player. It was therefore felt that intelligence collection should concentrate on the company itself by means of telephone discussions with staff and if possible a visit. Once activated, this approach fell foul of a common problem in small companies, namely, that all incoming calls were screened by an administrative assistant and that it was impossible to dial directly to any individual staff member. The 'gatekeeper' relayed messages and requests for interviews to contacts within the company but always came back with a refusal.

A third line of attack, using published sources, was being implemented at the same time as the requests for interviews and yielded a copy of the annual reports and accounts and a series of articles in the local press. The annual reports provided all of the financial background on the company plus a limited amount of information on the container linings business. Profits looked good but the company had not grown in the years preceding the investigation. The local press reports showed the reason for the sensitivity within the company and led the research team to decide that further direct approaches would be fruitless at that time. The founder of the company had recently died and two sons and a daughter had inherited the company. Only one son had worked previously in the company but after the father's death the second son had joined him. The daughter remained outside the business. The sons had made statements to the effect that they were going to develop the company and maintain the family tradition, which may have been true but is often code for 'we are fattening up the company for sale'.

The research team decided that there were two options at this point. The first was to recommend to the client that they make a direct approach to the target and ask whether a sale would be considered. The second was to carry on collecting data before an approach was made. The client decided that they needed more data before making an approach and the only method by which this could be achieved was to carry out a screening exercise amongst companies that could be doing business with the target and interview anyone who knew them. A painstaking programme involving a large number of short screening calls to procurement managers in bridge-building and engineering companies across Europe eventually identified a small number that were buying from the target company and an even smaller number that had recently been approached by their sales representative. From these it was found that the company was indeed trying to expand its client base and was making presentations about its services, its solution development skills, its advanced production facilities and its existing clients. One of the contacts that had been approached provided a copy of the presentation materials and these not only answered some of the intelligence topics but also provided the identities of more customers. From here the investigation picked up speed until a components buyer in a major engineering group, when asked whether he knew the target company, replied, 'Sure, I think we have just bought them!' The sales programme activated by the target had led them to the door of a buyer for the company. The follow-up was swift and conclusive and the investigation was halted.

Although the data collection process was highly successful, the outcome was unsatisfactory in that the client failed to make an acquisition. The loss was made worse by the fact that the data showed that the company could have been a good acquisition at that time!

Filling the Gaps in an Incomplete Picture

There is very little magic that can be applied to the task of filling gaps in an incomplete set of data. Most analysts rely on common sense, triangulations of data from various sources, comparisons with their own experience, comparisons between competitor companies, estimations and guesswork. At its most basic this type of analysis relies on deductions of the kind which says if A equals X and B equals Y then

C must equal Z. However, the more advanced analysis will use comparative data to show:

- What are the outside limits of data that could be reasonably expected
- What is the likely point within the range that applies to this particular company

In making these deductions spreadsheets have mechanised hand analysis and speeded the process to the extent that it is possible to run large numbers of alternative observations and arrive at a 'most likely' deduction in a short period of time. The spreadsheet approach is, in effect, a model of the business that uses simple ratios to determine whether the data make sense. For example if independently derived sales and employee data result in a sales per employee ratio that is outside the norms for that business then one or other of the numbers is suspect and needs to be re-examined.

The first problem with this type of analysis is that it tends to make the results for all companies analysed conform to assumed norms for the business. As a starting point this is acceptable but the real task of competitor intelligence is to show what is *different* about each competitor. It is at this stage that original data are required, even if they only provide a hint at whether a company is better or worse at a particular function than the rest of the industry. As stated in the opening paragraphs, the investigative process needs to hold time in reserve for carrying out more interviews at this stage so that any deductions can be tested with respondents. It is much easier to test deduced facts for reasonableness than it is to ask for them outright.

Paradoxically, problems can also arise when the data that have been obtained are too voluminous. Fitting large numbers of fragments into a coherent pattern can be far more difficult than dealing with small numbers of facts. The main danger arises from the possibility of adding error to error and arriving at a result that is too far from the truth to be useful. This is not an argument for limiting the amount of data collected, only a warning that volume is not necessarily a method of improving accuracy.

Extending the Level of Understanding

At the apex of the analytical skills required in competitive intelligence are those required to interpret results to identify competitors' intentions. This can never be a precise activity and is a high form of art rather than a science. It involves bringing together the full range of data that have been collected and using them as a basis for deduction. Whether, in the words of Sherlock Holmes, it is 'a two pipe or a four pipe' task depends on the importance attached to the conclusions but there is no doubt that extended thinking time, brainstorming and internal workshops will normally provide better results.

A range of quasi-scientific approaches have been used for the purpose of deducing competitors' intentions but in many cases the science obscures the fact that the foundations on which the deductions are based are very shaky and can lead to conclusions that have a spurious level of accuracy. One of the basic rules of research, garbage in–garbage out, applies strongly in the case of competitive intelligence. A process that works well is one in which the analysts:

- Establish a set of hypotheses
- Use parallel teams to evaluate them
- Recycle hypotheses externally
- Check fit of new data as they emerge
- Run 'what if?' analysis

Establish hypotheses

The first task is to establish a range of hypotheses that could fit the facts that have been revealed by the research. In the unlikely event that there is only one hypothesis that fits there is a possibility that it is close to the truth. More normally there are several interpretations that fit the facts to varying extents. The degree of fit can be used as a basis for assigning a probability to each hypothesis. In forming the hypotheses the key inputs are:

- Current situation – what is the marketing, production and financial situation of the company?
- Problems – what are the key problems that the competitor is facing?
- Pressures – what pressures are being placed on the company to improve performance or correct problems?
- Past trends – what is the history of the competitors' activities and how successful have they been in resolving problems and meeting objectives?
- Personality profiles – what is the track record of the management team and how have they faced up to problems in the past?
- Resources – what resources does the competitor have at its disposal?

When considering the data it is essential to remember that the past is a guide to the future only if there are no significant changes within the organisation or in the competitive environment in which it is operating. Forecasting by reference exclusively to the past is like driving a car looking only in the rear-view mirror – it works until you come to a bend! Although company cultures tend to change on a relatively long time-scale, events can occur that cause a significant break with the past. Fortunately, these are normally quite visible and include changes of ownership, changes of senior personnel and diversifications into new business sectors.

Parallel teams

Having established the hypotheses it is necessary to evaluate them, eliminating those that are highly unlikely and deciding which of the alternatives are most likely to describe competitor actions. Whilst competitor analysts can do this themselves to an extent, by this time they are so immersed in the data that they will find it increasingly difficult to take an objective view. They are also likely to lack operational experience in day-to-day decision-making. It is therefore useful to increase the evaluation team to include operational management. They can be given the task of placing themselves in their competitors' shoes in order to determine what they would do if confronted with a similar set of facts. The process needs to include a certain amount of role playing since there is little point in the executives being themselves. They must project themselves into their competitors' cultures and react accordingly.

The output from the parallel teams is likely to be:

- A shorter list of hypotheses
- New hypotheses that may be hybrids of the original set
- Hypotheses that are favoured for further analysis

Recycle hypotheses externally

Once they have been subjected to scrutiny by staff the hypotheses can then be tested with external observers who are thought to be in a position to comment. In the case of public companies these could be analysts working for the stockbrokers that follow the companies. In the case of private companies the closest that it may be possible to get are partners, distributors or major customers, though in all three cases there is a risk that the results of the evaluation will find their way back to the competitors being covered.

Check fit of new data as they emerge

The next step in the process is to monitor the progress of each company and determine the extent to which the moves that they make fit one or more of the favoured hypotheses. The dynamic element is vital not only as a method of determining whether the assumptions are correct but also as a means of refining them and reshaping them as the competitive situation evolves. Over time a single hypothesis should emerge as a logical explanation for the company's actions though the clarity with which this will be seen will depend on the amount of change that is occurring in the competitive environment. Like all other suppliers, competitors have to respond to environmental change and this is likely to alter their tactics and possibly their strategic approach.

Run 'what if?' analysis

The development of a model that explains competitor behaviour is useful only if it is used. One of the most useful applications is to run 'what if?' analyses, which use the model to predict competitor behaviour in the event of assumed circumstances. To be effective for these applications the model needs to include characteristics that define the behaviour of management. These could include such fundamentals as confidence, insecurity, arrogance, humility, subtlety, aggression and passiveness, which determine whether the company is likely to fight its way through problems or retreat from them.

Environmental Analysis

No competitive intelligence programme can be complete without an analysis of the competitive environment. To a very large extent this overlaps with market and economic analysis. It includes all factors that can influence the evolution of competitive activity, such as:

- Changes in customer requirements
- Growth or decline in satisfaction with competitors' offers
- Awareness of new competitors
- Demand changes
- Structural changes in distribution
- Changes in technology

- Changes in costs and pricing
- The development of the macroeconomic environment

Programmes for tracking these factors are well-established in most large companies, mainly within the market research department and all that is necessary is to make them accessible to the competitor analysts.

11 Verifying Intelligence

As with all data, competitive intelligence needs to be accurate to be useful. Unfortunately, by its very nature competitive intelligence is prone to be inaccurate. This is partly because it is difficult to obtain complete information but also because inaccurate intelligence about competitors' activities circulates widely in all markets and is often accepted as fact. The rumour mill works hard on news about companies, particularly when the news is adverse. It therefore essential that careful checks are made to ensure that errors are minimised. It is also essential that when the checks are completed the probable quality of the intelligence is assessed and is clearly stated in any reports issued. To do this requires the use of verification procedures that are applied during the data collection process and retrospectively once the intelligence has been analysed. These procedures are particularly important for intelligence obtained from the Internet but also applies for that obtained from other secondary sources and even from primary sources.

Verification of Published Intelligence

The basic checks that should be carried out should cover the following attributes of each item of data:

- Author
- Publisher
- Date
- Purpose
- Methodology
- Cross-checks
- Internet

Author

The identity of the author, be it an individual or an organisation, is the primary indicator of the authenticity and accuracy of intelligence. The easiest to check are known names whose other work can be read. Prolific publishers of intelligence, such as major research companies, are likely to have a reputation that can be checked by reference to other users. However, the fact that an author is unknown does not make the work inaccurate; it just means that the verification process is more complex. The signals of authenticity are:

- The provision of complete provenance and contact details on the author; a desire for anonymity is a sign of potential problems
- References to the author in other documents, which suggests that others have used the work and found it to be accurate
- Biographical details and experience statements, which permit the reader to judge the level of authority from which the author is writing
- Attribution of data that have been extracted from other secondary sources which is an indication that the author takes the research process seriously

Authors who are employed by the company which the intelligence covers can generally be regarded as being more accurate than those who derive the intelligence from third parties or secondary sources. In-house authors are more likely to know the truth and are unlikely to have much desire to mislead any customers that might read what they have written.

Publisher

If the publisher of the data is different from the author, the publisher's identity can help authenticate the data. As with authors, known publishers with an established track record and a reputation for quality are generally more trustworthy than unknown publishers. If the publisher is unknown, the availability of information on who they are and how they can be located provides an opportunity to check up on them either directly or by seeking information from others that may have used their data.

Publication date

As with any information, the date it was published shows its currency. Statistics are usually (though not always) tied to specific dates but technical information and company data lose value as they age. Intelligence users should therefore check the publication date of any document consulted.

Purpose

It is useful to establish the reason for which intelligence has been published. Government and international organisation publications that set out to provide factual information are likely to be reasonably accurate. However, there could be a significant difference in objectivity between a document published by a government statistical service, which is designed only to inform, and one published by a government tourist authority which is designed to attract visitors. Company publications have an obvious promotional purpose which means that although it is unlikely that the data they contain will be knowingly inaccurate, they may be slanted to place the company in the most favourable light with potential clients. This may lead to a level of exaggeration or to the use of broad statements that are ambiguous. Broker's reports published by a company's official broker may lose some of their objectivity in their enthusiasm to please their employers and boost share prices.

Methodology

The provision of details on how the data in a publication have been collected is a primary indication of quality and authenticity. Data that have been collected by techniques that are fully described have more credibility than a set of facts or statements whose origins are completely unknown.

Cross-checks

The ultimate test of authenticity is whether the data cross-check with similar data obtained from other sources. Similar data sets arising from a number of independent sources suggests accuracy, though it is always possible that inaccurate data emanating from a single source are being picked up and broadcast by a number of independent publishers. This is common in the newspaper world where different journals pick up and publish the same press release without checking its accuracy. Unfortunately facts gain in stature the more frequently they are published, regardless of their accuracy.

Intelligence from the Internet

Verification of the information available from Internet sites is essential. There is no control over what is placed on the Internet and although a high proportion of what can be accessed is accurate and useful there is also a considerable amount of rubbish. The openness of the Internet means that it attracts a large number of cranks who use it as a low-cost way of seeing their name in print. This means that researchers using the Internet need to develop a mechanism for checking the quality of the information they have identified.[1]

The ease with which anyone can put up a website on a host system means that there is no cost barrier that might deter the more spurious Internet publishers. Use of a host organisation does not necessarily indicate poor quality but publishers who run their own server are easier to check up on. It is also likely that personal web pages are more dubious in quality than organisational pages. Documents which are 'self-published' have always been more suspect than those that have gone through the hands of a recognised publisher.

The most reliable intelligence to be obtained from the Internet is that which is obtained from:

- Company websites
- Government websites
- Commercial databases
- The websites of educational establishments

Those that should be treated with more suspicion are:

- Websites created for political purposes
- Pressure group websites
- Corporate attack websites

These websites have a purpose that could well compromise their objectivity and cause them to distort the intelligence they provide. A prime example is websites created by ex-employees whose main purpose is to disseminate intelligence that places their former employer in the poorest possible light. The same applies to sites that purport to publish facts about companies that other media refuse to publish. The refusal may be based on the fact that the publisher is worried about a libel case but it could also be that they know the data are wrong.

Verification of Primary Intelligence

Primary intelligence requires an even greater amount of verification than secondary intelligence. It is far easier for respondents to make misleading or inaccurate statements than it is to write them. The verification of primary intelligence relies on establishing:

- The identity and job function of the information provider
- The circumstances in which the intelligence is obtained
- The degree of security surrounding the company or the type of intelligence being sought
- Corroboration from independent sources

Identity and job function of the intelligence provider

Obviously, any intelligence provider must be in a position to know the information being elicited. Information diffuses throughout companies and it is possible for relatively low-level staff to be in a position to pass on accurate intelligence but it is also possible for them to have heard information that is distorted or which they distort themselves. It is therefore necessary to balance the need to speak to sources that may be less guarded in what they reveal against the possibility that their knowledge is inaccurate.

When collecting primary intelligence a careful log must be kept of all calls and conversations showing:

- Name, company and telephone number of each respondent
- Respondent's stated job function
- The relationship between the respondent and the company being studied (for example, employee, supplier or distributor)
- The date and time of the conversation
- The intelligence provided
- An assessment of the difficulty of extracting the intelligence from the respondent (for example, willing respondent or highly suspicious)

Apart from the potential need to recontact respondents, the importance of the log is that when looking back it is often impossible to remember the circumstances surrounding each call that was made. Yet these data will be extremely useful if there is a need to decide whether intelligence from one source is likely to be more accurate than intelligence from another.

Circumstances in which the intelligence is obtained

The circumstances in which intelligence is obtained provide a further indication of accuracy. The ideal situations are those in which the respondents have no reason to suspect the motives for the enquiry and are evidently unguarded. The most worrying are those in which the respondents display a high level of suspicion and reluctance to talk. The latter are usually poor sources of intelligence anyway but there is an added risk that they will seek to deceive by providing misinformation.

Examples of ideal situations are encounters engineered at conferences and exhibitions and intelligence that is obtained by direct observation. That which the analyst has seen personally is likely to be more reliable than intelligence conveyed exclusively by word of mouth. The more difficult situations are invariably those in which employees are telephoned directly for intelligence and where the reason for the request cannot be clearly defined.

Security surrounding the company or type of intelligence

Some companies are naturally more suspicious than others. Suspicion may be a consequence of the business sector in which they operate (for example, defence), the level of competition they encounter, the fact that they are actively involved in competitive intelligence themselves or a management culture that discourages contact with any part of the outside world that is not a customer or a supplier. High levels of suspicion normally mean that the intelligence yield will be low but they may also indicate that any information that is obtained might be distorted.

The type of intelligence being sought may itself cause respondents to dissemble in their responses. Whilst there are many questions that respondents would regard as being reasonable, such as those covering products, supply conditions and even prices, there are others where an employee would find it difficult to understand why an outsider would want information unless they were carrying out an intelligence programme. It is common for a conversation with a competitor to proceed amicably up to the point at which a question on a sensitive topic is asked and for it then to cease because the questioner has stepped over a boundary line and into territory that the respondent regards as being confidential to the company. A conversation that is terminated represents no problem other than an inability to obtain the intelligence. Dangers arise if the respondent continues the conversation but gives misleading replies to questions. Intelligence gatherers need to be well tuned in to the mood of the conversations they have with competitors so that they can detect potential problems of this sort. The most obvious signals of problems are the questions that are asked. 'Wait a minute, what are you collecting this information for?' or 'Tell me again, who are you doing this survey for?' are clear indications that the respondent's receptivity to questions has changed for the worse.

Corroboration from independent sources

The most valid check on all intelligence is the extent to which the facts are either repeated consistently by several sources or where different facts all point to the same conclusion. It is possible for a group of respondents to sing the same inaccurate song providing they use the same song sheet but it is unlikely that companies would go to such lengths to mislead their competitors unless they felt they were under an intense competitive intelligence attack.

Seeking intelligence from multiple sources is a basic tenet of competitive intelligence and care must always be taken with data obtained from companies that direct all requests for intelligence to a single source. Commonly this is the department for 'Public Affairs' whose task is not only to provide information about the company but also to limit the outflow to that which is essential.

Sanity Checks

The final check on all data is that of 'reasonableness': not only 'whether it fits with all the other facts that have been obtained' but also 'whether it is reasonable' in the light of general company and industry norms. This is easiest to see with performance data where sets of figures result in averages, such as sales per employee or output per member of the workforce, that are unlikely. Testing whether intelligence is reasonable is easier if several competitors are studied simultaneously and when data for the commissioning company are available (providing they are in the same business). This provides a multiplicity of observations that can be compared.

Note

1. For further information see the writings of Elizabeth E. Kirk to be found through the ResearchInfo.com Internet site.

12 Competitive Intelligence Resources

A key decision facing all companies developing competitive strategies is how to collect, analyse and disseminate the intelligence they require. As with market research the options are to establish a competitive intelligence department, to use external intelligence collection agencies, or a combination of the two.

In-House Resources or External Agencies

In-house competitive intelligence departments have a number of advantages but are not suitable for all companies or for all types of intelligence. The most obvious advantage of an in-house department is that they develop a high level of expertise in the business in which the company is operating, they become very familiar with the competitors, can build up a range of intelligence sources, can develop a network of contacts and can continuously track developments. They can therefore obtain intelligence relatively efficiently and quickly. Their main disadvantage is the difficulties they face when collecting primary intelligence. Under the rules of engagement they must identify themselves and their employer when speaking with sources and this places a severe constraint on the questions they can expect to get answered. In smaller companies there is an added problem that arises from the fact that there may not be sufficient demand for intelligence to keep even one specialist busy full-time. If employed they may be used only because they are there, rather than because their services are genuinely required. The compromise solution for those organisations that do not require a complete intelligence facility but do not wish to dispense completely with an in-house research resource, is to employ a competitive or business intelligence manager.[1] Their role would be to collect internal and secondary intelligence and fill the gaps by employing external suppliers whose main strength is primary intelligence gathering. The final option is to use external specialists for all intelligence provision.

Outsourcing offers a number of advantages which in-house services find it difficult to replicate. The most important of these are:

- Anonymity
- Objectivity
- Cross-fertilisation
- Intermittent services
- Cost savings

Anonymity

In any primary intelligence-gathering programme it is essential that the identity of the company planning to use the data remains confidential. In-house departments cannot disguise their identity but external suppliers are under no obligation to reveal the name of the client that has employed them.

Anonymity is also a method of increasing the objectivity of the intelligence provided by respondents. Knowledge of who the intelligence is for may well encourage respondents to distort their responses.

Objectivity

All intelligence needs to be objective and unbiased if it is to be useful. It also needs to be *seen to be* unbiased. Internal intelligence resources risk being exposed to internal opinions on competitors and the fact that these may colour their findings. This danger is particularly true when the facts that are gathered are thin on the ground and can be made to fit a number of different interpretations. An external intelligence agency can be isolated from the internal cross-currents of opinion about competitors and the results they present can be shown to be free of any bias.

Cross-fertilisation

Internal competitive intelligence analysts develop valuable expertise in their industry sector which may improve the efficiency of the research process and the depth of analysis. However, an external agency generally sees many different industries and is in a position to import new thinking and fresh solutions.

Intermittent services

An external competitive intelligence agency can be employed only when required. The continuous availability of internal research staff may lead to the generation of low-priority problems to keep them busy.

Cost savings

By not imposing a continuous overhead burden on the company the use of external intelligence agencies tends to incur lower costs than the maintenance of an internal department. More importantly, agencies that specialise in competitive intelligence develop skills that result in a more efficient and therefore less time-consuming process.

The Internal Competitive Intelligence Organisation

Despite the growing use of competitive intelligence there are very few internal competitive intelligence departments that have more than one or two employees. Large departments exist only in companies for whom detailed knowledge of competitors is deemed to be critical to their performance. This exists in certain industries such as pharmaceuticals and financial services where the investment in new products is high and the shape and structure of the competitive landscape are changing rapidly.

For efficiency, the competitive intelligence function either lies within the market research function or is a separate unit within a general market or business intelligence department. Occasionally it may also be allied with the information department or corporate library. However it is structured organisationally, competitive intelligence staff rarely divide their time between the study of markets and the study of competitors. Competitive intelligence is a specialisation that demands a different skill set and it does not mix with the quantitative and qualitative research skills of the market researcher.

The reporting channels for competitive intelligence are also different to those for market research. For better or worse market research is fed primarily to line product development and marketing staff. Competitive intelligence can be fed down the same channels but is far more likely to be transmitted directly to strategic management and board members. In a number of major competitive intelligence users the reporting line is direct to the Managing Director or CEO.

A typical full-scale competitive intelligence department in a large company contains the following resources:

- Competitive intelligence manager
- Competitive analysts
- Information specialists
- Support personnel

Between them these can handle all of the liaison and research functions that are suitable for internal staff, including:

- Identifying the intelligence requirements of various departments of the business
- Assessing the importance of the intelligence objectives and the feasibility of meeting them
- Producing a list of key intelligence topics
- Liaising with the legal department to ensure compliance with legal requirements
- Carrying out secondary research
- Establishing an internal competitive intelligence network
- Collecting intelligence from internal sources on a systematic basis
- Establishing an external network of contacts that can provide intelligence
- Maintaining a list of agencies that can provide competitive intelligence that cannot be acquired from secondary sources, internal contacts and external networks
- Ensuring that agencies comply with the company's ethical guidelines
- Briefing external agencies for projects
- Liaising with external agencies during projects
- Receiving reports from external agencies and ensuring that the brief has been fulfilled
- Building a database of intelligence and maintaining it
- Filtering competitive intelligence from all sources and issuing results to selected staff by means of reports, a newsletter, an intranet site or a competitive intelligence system
- Interpreting intelligence and producing strategic analyses on competitors
- Collecting follow-up questions and new intelligence requirements and initiating a new round of the intelligence collection process

As the above sequence implies, competitive intelligence tasks run in loops that never end. Each round of intelligence collection, each new set of facts, each change in the competitive environment breeds new tasks.

Competitive Intelligence Staff

Establishing and running a competitive intelligence unit requires staff that are capable of delivering results. As indicated above, the range of tasks is extremely diverse and the availability of trained candidates is limited. There is no shortage of people that would like to work in competitive intelligence but the proportion of them that are suitable is very low. The ideal competitive intelligence employee requires a unique basket of skills that include:

- Data collection – the ability to take a patient semi-academic approach when looking for secondary sources and then match that with an aggressive approach on the telephone or face-to-face when seeking primary intelligence
- Resourcefulness – the ability to devise unique methods of obtaining data after all the obvious routes have failed
- Persistence – never giving up on a project until all avenues have been tried
- Insensitivity – the ability to withstand constant rejection
- Inquisitiveness – a genuine love of problems and the search for solutions
- Clarity – the ability to see through complex and often conflicting sets of data
- Analysis – good pattern recognition ability and the ability to infer relationships between disparate facts
- Sound business sense and a basic knowledge of financial analysis
- Communication – the ability to listen to the requirements of intelligence users and convert them into an intelligence brief then communicate the findings in written documents and orally
- Systems – the ability to install and run a system for intelligence distribution
- Discretion

Although some of the best competitive intelligence analysts combine all of these skills, it is more likely that for a fully functioning department a team of analysts will need to be formed – some with skills in intelligence gathering, some with analytical and interpretative skills and some with communication skills.

Within companies the choice when searching for competitive intelligence staff is to seek them from within or to recruit from the outside. Internal candidates have the advantage of knowing both the company and the industry in which it operates. This is extremely useful but does not override the personal characteristics that make a good competitive analyst. Looking outside the company is an option but the pool of trained competitive intelligence staff is small and it is likely that the result of an external recruitment exercise will be a novice that appears to have the right personal qualities but no relevant experience.

The activities in which suitable candidates for competitive intelligence roles might be found are:

- Market research – the data collection and analytical skills of market researchers can be readily adapted to competitive intelligence
- Strategic, business and market planning
- Police – support specialists rather than police officers
- Military intelligence
- Security services

A large number of competitive intelligence analysts have entered the business after an initial career in the security intelligence services. The training they receive in intelligence collection and interpretation translates very readily into the gentler art of competitive intelligence even if some of the interrogation techniques used by the security services do not. Former police officers are a different matter. They tend to find that the transition, from the ability to force responses to questions to a situation in which responses have to be solicited gently, is difficult to manage. Police training is better employed on company security rather than competitive intelligence.

Identifying Potential External Suppliers

The steps in identifying potential research companies are reasonably straightforward. The first is to obtain a list of specialists in competitive intelligence that identifies:

- The types of service they offer, notably secondary, primary or both
- Their skills and experience in specific product or industry sectors
- Their size (personnel and sales)
- The countries they cover

It is also tempting to ask for a list of previous clients, but do not expect an answer. All intelligence gathering is done on a confidential basis usually supported by non-disclosure agreements under which agencies agree to maintain the confidentiality of their clients, even to the extent of not revealing their names.

Because of the nature of the work, competitive intelligence tends to be a relatively secretive world, a characteristic that is enhanced to an extent by the fact that a number of practitioners have entered the business from government intelligence agencies and there are many others that make a fetish of secrecy. It can therefore be quite difficult to identify suitable agencies. The most valuable source of a list of competitive intelligence agencies is the membership directory of the Society of Competitive Intelligence Professionals (SCIP): most, though not all, agencies employ members of SCIP and are therefore listed in the directory. For inclusion in the SCIP lists members must subscribe to the SCIP Code of Ethics. This provides a safeguard that, if used, the members will not engage in practices that are likely to get their clients into a situation that will result in adverse publicity. SCIP publications also carry advertisements for competitive intelligence agencies but these are rarely carried in the general marketing press and buyers' guides for marketing services.

An Internet search using the words 'competitive intelligence' will identify some 9000 sites, many of which are the websites of vendors of various types of intelligence-gathering services. Others are listings of competitive intelligence services and information about competitive intelligence of varying degrees of sophistication and usefulness. Company listings on the Internet need to be treated with some caution since they often contain only those organisations that have registered with the site operator. This is not to say that the companies listed are unsuitable, only that the lists are likely to be incomplete. A further problem with websites is that they provide ample illustration of the old adage that 'empty vessels make the most noise'. It is commonly the case that sole practitioners establish websites of some substance in order to suggest that they have sizeable organisations.

Each year there are a number of conferences on competitive intelligence at which practitioners speak. Some are regular fixtures, such as the annual US and European conferences organised by SCIP, and others are organised on an *ad hoc* basis by professional conference organisers. Although the latter tend to ebb and flow in frequency depending on the level of interest in the subject, they are used by competitive intelligence companies as a method of showcasing their services and specialisations and therefore provide an opportunity to see them in action.

It is always worth asking known users of competitive intelligence, trade associations and business consultants (including the Business Links) for qualified suggestions on suitable intelligence agencies. This is an excellent method in that anyone recommending an agency should also be in a position to identify their strengths and weaknesses.

Finally, a number of competitive intelligence agencies actively promote their services by direct mail. Rather than consign such material to the waste bin, it is worth reading and filing for future reference when a need arises. Active promotion suggests that an agency has confidence in its services and should be worth considering.

Assessing the Suitability of Competitive Intelligence Agencies

Many of the normal methods of assessing the suitability of a service provider do not work when it comes to competitive intelligence. A reputable agency will not reveal the names of clients they have worked for nor will they show examples of reports they have written. As all of their work is custom-designed to meet the specific needs of each client's specific requirements, they are not able to show general studies that provide some tangible evidence of their ability to obtain high-quality intelligence. Nevertheless, there are other indicators of apparent suitability. The most important of these are:

- Ethical standards
- Size and organisational structure
- Personnel
- Language
- Understanding
- Supervision and control
- Apparent compatibility with the client organisation
- Track record
- Conflicts of interest
- References
- Premises
- Responsiveness
- Brochures and Internet sites

Ethical standards

Before considering any other aspect of a competitive intelligence agency's operations it is essential to establish the ethical standards by which they operate. This applies primarily to the techniques they are prepared to use and the basis on which they are prepared to collect intelligence. The ethics of legitimate competitive intelligence collection are set out at length in Chapter 15 and agencies that are prepared to ignore these guidelines can cause their clients severe embarrassment. The acid test is whether they would do anything that their client would not like to see reported in the media and could not defend if challenged. In initial discussions it is worth establishing the types of intelligence the agency would not be comfortable trying to collect. In other words, when does the agency say 'no'? Agencies that claim to be able to collect highly confidential intelligence should be avoided since they are likely to be using techniques that are either unethical or illegal.

Size and organisational structure

Competitive intelligence is a business into which the cost of entry is low. This results in a proliferation of sole practitioners and small companies working alongside medium-sized companies. Within the normal definition of the term, there are no large competitive intelligence agencies. The size and legal format of the organisation say little about its suitability to carry out any individual project, but it is essential to recognise that not all organisations will have the skills and resources to carry out projects equally well. A small specialist unit may be ideal if they have directly relevant experience and/or the top person is going to devote a high proportion of his or her time to the project. Even so, companies with substantial resources and a broad range of skills may be better positioned to carry out large complex projects.

There is a perennial question about whether it is better to be a big fish in a little pond or a little fish in a relatively big pond. The advantage of being a major client of an agency is that it will normally result in preferential treatment. No agency wants to lose a major source of business and will tend to perform consistently well to ensure that this does not happen. The size of company in which this can be achieved depends entirely on the volume of business that is to be placed.

Personnel

The quality of all projects is dependent on the professionals that will carry them out. A primary indicator of suitability is their educational background and their experience in intelligence collection. Particular attention should be paid to the senior staff assigned to the account since it is their abilities, even more than those of the executives, that will determine the quality of the project. Beware of professional sales representatives who have a high order of skill but will vanish off the scene as soon as a contract is placed. They have a role to play but may not have the time or the ability to influence the quality of the project.

Supervision and control

The level of involvement of the management of the agency in the conduct of the survey is an important indicator of quality. Most clients will be best serviced by an organisation that involves its senior staff in the specification of the research, monitoring progress and the interpretation of the findings. Indications of excessive delegation to junior staff should be treated as a serious warning signal.

Language

Agencies that make excessive use of security jargon and military anecdotes should be viewed with caution. It suggests that they see a close association between the worlds of military and competitive intelligence and may be somewhat cavalier in the techniques they are prepared to use on behalf of their clients.

Understanding

It should be clear from the first encounter that the agency fully understands that obtaining competitive intelligence is not an easy task and that there are certain types of intelligence that may prove impossible to get. They should also show that they realise that an intelligence programme should be stopped if it becomes evident that it will not succeed. There is little point in wasting a client's budget on seeking the unobtainable.

Compatibility

The research process requires considerable interaction between the client and the agency. The primary contact in the agency therefore needs to be a person who not only has the appropriate level of skill but also commands the confidence and respect of the client as well as being sensitive to the client's requirements.

Track record

Relevant experience can be an important indicator since it is likely to shorten the learning curve within the agency and will enable them to bring a higher level of industry knowledge to the problem. Although agencies cannot reveal the nature of specific projects in which they have been involved they should be able to state the sectors in which they have extensive experience and be able to support that by talking knowledgeably about each sector. However, it is important to distinguish between the experience of the company and that of the individuals within it. Company experience may be irrelevant if the individuals that gained it have left. Individual experience is relevant regardless of the company within which it was gained.

Conflicts of interest

High levels of expertise in a sector may mean that an agency has potential conflicts of interest. Unlike other research services, it is difficult for an agency to work for more than one client in a sector. In order to be effective agencies need to be party to intelligence about their client's operations and aspirations, and it must be perfectly clear that there is absolutely no risk that this will fall into the hands of competitors. This is difficult to guarantee if an agency works for direct competitors. The exception is where sectors are so fragmented that they can be treated as a number of separate businesses. Pharmaceutical companies compete but are not necessarily active in the same therapeutic areas. It is therefore possible for an agency to work for a number of pharmaceutical companies but on separate therapies.

References

No competitive intelligence agency should volunteer a list of previous clients. However, if required, they should be able to persuade some previous clients to provide references for them. However, when considering these it should be remembered that agencies will refer potential clients only to their successes, not their failures.

Premises

A visit to the agencies' premises will show whether the physical resources of the company appear to match their written or oral statements. A visit permits observation of the approximate number of staff, the type of staff employed, the corporate culture and the quality and organisation of the premises. Lavish premises can be variously interpreted. They may indicate that the organisation is successful, believes that a good working environment is conducive to quality workmanship and that it looks after its staff. It may also suggest that the fees are high. Poor-quality premises may suggest that the fees will be low but also that the quality of the research output will also be low.

Responsiveness

A company will be at its best when in the process of winning business; any shortfalls in responsiveness at this stage could indicate that there will be more serious delays once assignments are actually commissioned.

Brochures and Internet sites

Sales literature has to be treated with caution but its quality and content say something about the company. Poor brochure material is probably more significant than high-quality documentation. It is relatively easy to put a good brochure together and a company that is not concerned with brochure quality may not be committed to the overall quality of its service.

Internet sites are also easy to construct but a number of companies use them as an opportunity to demonstrate their expertise. A simple, well-designed and interesting site can be equally as effective as a good brochure but the Internet provides an opportunity to extend data provision to include white papers on competitive intelligence techniques and applications and other material which can boost confidence in the company's abilities.

Compiling a Shortlist

The review of intelligence agencies should be used to compile a shortlist of potential suppliers who are apparently capable of carrying out intelligence exercises satisfactorily. The shortlist should contain a maximum of three or four agencies – any more will impose a heavy burden when briefing potential suppliers, will tend to be confusing during the evaluation of proposals and is unfair to the intelligence agencies, given the effort required from them in the next stages of the selection process. Furthermore, intelligence agencies will tend to put far more effort into the preparation of their proposals if they have a one-in-three or -four chance of success, rather than a lottery involving tens of suppliers.

The shortlist will tend to gravitate towards companies that appear to have the right background but it is advantageous to select companies of different sizes and types since they are likely to construct different approaches.

Approved Research Contractors

It can be advantageous to seek a meeting before a brief is issued or even at a stage when no specific research project is in mind. Companies intending to use intelligence collection services regularly should have a list of agencies they could use and which covers all of the skills and resources they are likely to require. Some companies that contain a number of divisions that could commission research projects go as far as having an approved list of suppliers from which all vendors have to be chosen. Vetting suitable intelligence agencies is a time-consuming process, which should be repeated as little as possible. Educating intelligence agencies into the practices, ways of thinking and the specific requirements of an individual client is also a lengthy process which is best carried out with a limited number of potential suppliers but will pay major dividends in getting what is required. There is also a security problem. The more agencies that are briefed the greater the risk that information about a client's intelligence-gathering activities will leak into the outside world. Knowledge that a company uses market research has no value to its competitors; knowledge that a competitor engages in competitive intelligence is extremely valuable if only to ensure that counter intelligence techniques are fully deployed. Companies included in the shortlist of suppliers should all be asked to sign a blank non-disclosure agreement covering all information provided to them by the company.

The final stage in commissioning an intelligence project is the selection of the agency to use. Buying competitive intelligence is much like buying any other intangible service and has much in common with selecting market researchers, lawyers, accountants and management consultants. The main task is to select an organisation that is comfortable to work with and will deliver accurate intelligence at a price that matches the budget available.

The Proposal

Those invited to quote for intelligence projects should respond with a proposal that will be the basis for selection of the agency to be used. At its simplest in situations where the client has provided a very precise specification of what is required the proposal will contain the agencies' credentials, a response to any questions raised in the brief, suggestions for improving the project or reducing costs, and a fee.

Where the brief does little more than outline the problem the proposal needs to be much fuller and should contain:

- The intelligence objectives
- The intelligence topics to be covered
- An indication of the likely success in obtaining each item of intelligence
- The approach, the types of intelligence-gathering techniques to be deployed, the numbers of interviews and the intelligence sources to be targeted
- The methods by which the results will be presented to the client including the structure of the written report and the number and format of meetings
- The fee
- The time the process will take to complete
- The intelligence team and their qualifications
- Any related experience the agency has

It should be borne in mind that some agencies write better proposals than research documents, but the content, format, presentation and amount of thought provided in the proposal should give a reasonable guide to the ability of the agency.

When evaluating proposals there are a number of indications of the suitability and competence of the agencies that have prepared them. The most important is the amount of thought that has gone into the definition of the information to be sought and the methodology. Proposals that merely add a cost figure to the brief suggest that the agency has not given much thought to what is required and may not fully understand the problem. High levels of value added in the form of analysing the intelligence objectives, adding questions that will enhance the ability of the project to solve the specified problem and creative thought to the methods of obtaining the intelligence are all signs of an organisation that is not only competent but is genuinely interested in carrying out the project. Marks should also be given for a proposal that suggests alternative approaches which result in different costs – thus permitting the client to match the research with the budget that is available.

Assessing Alternative Offers

The primary yardsticks by which the quality and suitability of alternative offers should be assessed are:

- The degree to which the agency understands the competitive situation of the user and the purposes for which the intelligence is required
- The extent to which the offer meets the information requirements specified in the brief
- The extent to which the proposal shows that the agency has thought about the problem and has modified the approach and the intelligence yield to provide a better overall result for the client
- The proposed methodology for collecting intelligence and the likely success in achieving the intelligence objectives
- The extent to which the methodology is caveated – vague promises and caveats may be used as reasons why important items of intelligence are omitted from the report that is finally delivered
- Presentation – be wary of proposals that are double-spaced and printed on thick paper to give an impression of bulk
- Irrelevant content – be equally wary of proposals that contain a high proportion of standard and irrelevant content which is obviously designed to impress, is obviously included in all proposals but adds nothing to help the reader assess the suitability of the agency
- Language – the use of intelligence jargon, such as 'humint' and 'sigint' is often a sign that the agency has a perception of itself as bordering on the espionage business and may be prepared to use unethical techniques if the normal processes fail to provide a result
- The cost

Cost will be a primary consideration for most intelligence buyers and one aspect of proposals that sometimes surprises clients is the extreme variations in the cost that can be attached to alternative approaches. The cost of a research project is normally made up of a daily rate for executive time, overheads and expenses. In most countries, when comparing like for like, the costs tend to be very similar. This means that variations in cost can occur for a number of fundamental reasons including:

- The fact that the executives employed on the project are of differing levels of seniority and are remunerated at different rates – even sole practitioners can operate at significantly different daily fee rates depending on their experience and their confidence that they can persuade clients that they are worth higher rates
- An overhead structure that varies according to the levels of supervision and the costs of the staff and premises

- The varying efficiencies of the organisations, some working on a high intelligence yield per day and lower inputs of executive time than others that require more time input to achieve the same result
- Varying levels of profit expectations

Other factors that can cause significant variations in cost are:

- Differing interpretations of the difficulty of obtaining the intelligence that is sought
- The fact that some agencies may already have inside knowledge of the business which they will contribute to the solution
- The amount of contact time between agency and client that has been budgeted
- The desire, or lack of desire, to cost keenly in order to win the contract

Whilst the above can all be true, the most likely reason for variations in the cost of proposals produced in response to an identical brief is that the different agencies have interpreted the brief differently and are offering different solutions. This may not be obvious from the words contained in the proposal and before accepting a low-cost proposal, or dismissing one that is offered at a higher cost, it is well worth discussing the offers in detail in order to understand precisely what the differences are due to.

Presentation of Proposals

In the case of large complex assignments the intelligence agencies may be invited to present their proposals to the client organisation. This provides the agency with an opportunity to stress the reasons why they feel they are suited to carry out the exercise. It provides the client with an opportunity to ask further questions and test the statements made in the proposal.

Negotiations

A more acceptable but higher-cost proposal does not have to be accepted without negotiation. Professionals no longer place themselves in a position in which discussions of fees are avoided and there is always a deal to be done. Normally this will involve a compromise between trimming the methodology, trimming the intelligence yield and cutting the agency's profit margin.

Note

1. The job title given to in-house competitive intelligence managers can be critical. Although a title containing the words 'competitive intelligence' may be completely accurate it is not one that can be used outside the company when collecting data. The words Business Intelligence have therefore become a euphemism for Competitive Intelligence in many organisations.

13 The Intelligence Briefing

Obtaining competitive intelligence involves four key stages. They commence with the definition of the intelligence topics to be covered, as already discussed, and follow with a decision on who is to collect the intelligence, briefing them and obtaining a proposal, which is the internal analyst's or intelligence agency's response to the briefing they have been given.

An intelligence exercise is only as good as the initial brief. If intelligence users fail to set out what they require it is unlikely that the right result will be obtained. A good briefing, which may comprise a briefing document and a briefing meeting, flows naturally from the definition of the key intelligence topics but to ensure that the exercise is successful the analyst must be given more than a list of questions.

The Briefing Document

An intelligence brief needs to contain all of the information required to decide not only what intelligence is to be collected but also the potential sources of intelligence and the data collection methods that are to be used. Obviously the briefing document needs to be more comprehensive for external agencies but it is a mistake to assume that internal intelligence staff will automatically know all of the details required to ensure a good project. The content of the ideal intelligence brief should include:

- Background information
- The product or service to be covered
- The competitors to be covered and any relevant internally available information on them
- The overall objectives of the exercise

- Type of intelligence programme required
- Key intelligence topics
- Thoughts on the intelligence approach
- Documents
- Potential intelligence sources and contacts
- Exclusions from the intelligence process
- Confidentiality
- Timing
- Budgetary constraints
- Requirements from the agencies submitting proposals
- Date by which a proposal is expected
- Contacts within the client organisation
- Code of ethics

Background information

Background information should be given on any aspect of the company and its activities that could be relevant plus the market and competition situation in which the company operates. The need for background information will be greatest in the case of relatively unknown companies and highly specialised businesses which analysts are unlikely to have encountered before. Useful background information could include:

- An outline history of the company
- The nature of the market in which it operates
- The company's development within the business sector being covered
- The overall competitive environment
- The situation which has created the need for the intelligence

The product or service to be covered

The products or services to be covered by the exercise should be described in full. The description should cover:

- Product or service characteristics
- Applications
- Product or service strengths
- Distribution methods
- Users
- Known prices
- Points of differentiation between competitive products

The need for a detailed description is more important in the case of technical or specialised products or services. However, even in the case of well-known consumer items it may be helpful to describe the attributes of the product which have helped it gain its current market share and the methods by which competitors are believed to have achieved their positions within the market.

Competitors to be covered and relevant information

The brief should state which competitors are to be covered in the programme, the aspects of their services that are to be covered and any basic reference data that are already known. The latter may include their main locations, their products and services, segments of the market they are operating in and length of time in the business. Intelligence users are sometimes reluctant to hand over information they already hold on the grounds that the data may be played back to them or may bias the findings. However, there is little point in paying again for intelligence that already exists and is thought to be reasonably accurate. Anything that improves the efficiency of the intelligence collection process should be regarded as beneficial and it is far better to use the budget to collect new intelligence.

The overall objectives of the exercise

The objectives of the exercise must be clearly stated in terms that are as specific as possible. They should commence with a definition of the problem that has given rise to the need for intelligence (such as bidding for a major contract, planned introduction of a new product, entry into a new market, loss of market share, poor profit performance or suspected impending competitive action). The objectives should also state how intelligence is expected to help solve the problem (such as assisting tactical competitive decisions or providing the basis for an overall competitive strategy).

Type of intelligence programme

The brief should state the type of intelligence programme that is required, namely quick tactical intelligence gathering, competitor profiles or an on-going competitor-tracking exercise.

Key intelligence topics

The key intelligence topics specified by the intelligence user should be stated. At this stage the list can be as comprehensive as possible, though experienced intelligence users and others who have a feel for the magnitude of the task should ensure that the shopping list is likely to be achievable, given the difficulties of collecting intelligence, and is broadly consistent with time and budgetary constraints.

The topics should be prioritised so that the analysts know the items that are regarded as essential, those that are very useful and those that would be nice to have but not worth a special effort to obtain.

Thoughts on the intelligence approach

A high proportion of intelligence users have no contribution to make on the intelligence-gathering approach that should be adopted and nor should they. It is up to the professionals to convince users on the most effective, the most cost-efficient or the least-cost routes to obtaining intelligence. Nevertheless, there are areas on which users that know the business can comment and, in doing so, provide analysts with better insight on how intelligence can be collected. The most valuable contribution could be an analysis of the structure of the business and the types of organisations operating in it with an assessment of which types of organisation are likely to know most about the activities of competitors.

Documents

The brief can usefully include any documentation that is relevant. This normally includes brochures and catalogues but can be extended to internal reports and other evidence that might be helpful in orientating the agency preparing the proposal.

Potential external intelligence sources and contacts

The intelligence-gathering process normally requires as many contacts and references as possible. Intelligence users should therefore provide any assistance they can from their knowledge of the business, including:

- Potential sources of intelligence – this could include published sources, useful websites, employees that have worked previously for competitors, other staff that might have competitor knowledge, known staff of the competitors, and external contacts that might have knowledge of competitors' activities, such as trade association contacts, journalists or brokers' analysts that are known to have studied the competitors
- Opportunities to reach sources – such as forthcoming conferences, exhibitions or trade shows
- Related research already completed and potentially available
- Current industry issues that could be used by analysts as a method of initiating a dialogue with intelligence sources

Exclusions from the intelligence process

If there are organisations or individuals that should not be contacted in the exercise, for whatever reason, they should be identified in the brief.

Confidentiality

All competitive intelligence is carried out on a confidential basis and the results should remain the property of the sponsor. Requiring agencies to sign a non-disclosure agreement before sending them the briefing document may reinforce this. It is also reasonable to solicit an undertaking that an external agency will not carry out assignments for competitors for a defined period (18 months to two years) after the completion of the current project.

Timing

The brief should state clearly when the results of the exercise are required. Timing is always critical in competitive intelligence and the delivery of the results will often need to be tied in with other activities that are taking place. It is helpful for internal analysts and external agencies to know the overall timescale that is envisioned, such as:

- The dates by which the project is expected to be commissioned
- Key meetings during the programme
- The expected completion date
- The anticipated date for a discussion of the findings with the intelligence users

Even in the best-run companies these dates may slip for reasons which are nothing to do with the research, but knowing what is expected will enable the analyst to design an approach which will meet initial plans. The only word of warning is that tight sets of commissioning and delivery deadlines which are consistently missed soon earn companies reputations for not being serious.

Budgetary constraints

There are two diametrically opposed schools of thought on providing an indication of the budget in the briefing document. The first believes that agencies should be handed a problem and it is up to them to design and cost the most appropriate intelligence collection approach. The second thinks that the provision of an indicative budget will ensure that the approaches proposed are within the limits that the company can afford. If money is no object the first of these two alternatives poses no serious problems. Nor is it a problem if the intelligence user already has a reasonable idea from previous experience of what the exercise should cost. The problem arises with new competitive intelligence users who have no idea of what it can cost. For them an open-ended request for proposals will commonly result in surprises, usually unpleasant. Giving a budget indication avoids this problem, providing the budget is realistic. To get to this point the first-time intelligence user may need to do a little preparatory research on costs, part of which should be discussions with the intelligence agencies selected to submit proposals.

Requirements from the research companies submitting proposals

The brief should state any information that the client particularly requires the internal analyst or intelligence agency to include in the proposal. This could include:

- An indication of the feasibility of achieving the intelligence objectives
- An outline of previous experience in similar types of project
- A biographical note on the analysts who would carry out the exercise
- Organisations from which the client can seek references on the intelligence agency

Date by which a proposal is expected

As a separate item the briefing document should state when the proposal is required. Reasonable time should be permitted for proposal preparation, taking account of the fact that the analysts may require a meeting to discuss the project before preparing a proposal. Proposal writing, particularly for large, complex projects requiring preliminary research, can take a considerable amount of time but the norm lies between several hours and several days.

Contacts within the client organisation

Finally the brief should state the points of contact between the client organisation and the analysts. This should include the primary point of contact, to whom the proposal should be sent and to whom questions can be addressed.

Code of ethics

Many users of competitive intelligence have prepared codes of ethics that their own staff and external agencies working for them must adhere to. If these exist they should be sent with the briefing document.

The Briefing Meeting

The briefing document should be sent to agencies that have been shortlisted as capable of carrying out the project, together with an invitation to quote. Except in the case of the smallest and most straightforward intelligence requirements, the submission of a briefing document should be accompanied by an offer to meet with analysts to discuss the requirement in more depth. The meeting can take place at either the client's premises or the agency's offices. The former permits the client to invite additional staff members to discuss the requirement, to demonstrate products and to call for additional documentation; the latter provides an early opportunity for the client to see the analysts in their own environment.

The purpose of the briefing meeting is to provide an opportunity for the analysts to ask questions and to get the intelligence user to elaborate on the brief. It also enables the analyst to obtain a feel for the scale of the intelligence exercise that is expected, to obtain feedback on the likely acceptability of alternative approaches and to impress the client with his or her knowledge and competence. Both client and analyst should benefit from the exchange, the former by a better understanding of what is required and the latter through a deeper appreciation of what it is possible to obtain for the budget that is likely to be available.

A briefing meeting is an opportunity to observe agency personnel in action. The indicators of agency suitability that can be gained from the meeting are:

- The quality of the agency representative – he or she will tend to be one of their best staff and may not be typical of the rest of the team but if he or she is not good enough the remainder are unlikely to be better
- The level of market and industry knowledge that is displayed
- The apparent level of skill in competitive intelligence and the ability to explain the processes, the factors which determine the quality of the output and the compromises which may need to be made to achieve a result which is cost-effective for the client
- The level of honesty and the extent to which the agency will keep to ethical guidelines
- The extent to which the agency is prepared to be flexible to meet client requirements
- The commercial approach of the agency – an overtly 'hard nosed' commercial approach may indicate that the information will be superficial; an uncommercial, academic approach may indicate that the results will be too theoretical and unusable

14 Controlling the Intelligence Collection Process

Good intelligence results from an effective working relationship between intelligence users and intelligence gatherers, be they an internal department or an external agency. Each partner in the relationship must contribute the knowledge and skill that they derive from their respective backgrounds in order to get the most from the intelligence budget. Although it may be tempting to users to let the intelligence gatherers work to the brief and implement the project without interaction (or interfering), this can result in the outcome being less satisfactory. This is truest when working with outside intelligence agencies who are not party to the working culture within the commissioning company and do not have automatic or ready access to internally available intelligence.

Clients require skills in working with outside agencies so that they can make an effective contribution to the intelligence-gathering process. The steps by which clients can make an effective contribution to projects are:

- A full face-to-face briefing of the intelligence-gathering team prior to the commencement of the assignment
- Approval of any discussion guides that will be used during the primary intelligence-gathering activity
- Regular progress reports during the survey
- Regular reviews of the intelligence yield
- Final presentation of findings
- An independent assessment of the quality of the results

Project Briefing or 'Kick-Off' Meeting

At the commencement of all assignments the intelligence users should meet the entire intelligence-gathering team and brief them. In an ideal world these meetings should be in person but if this is not possible there should at least be telephone conference calls with enough time allowed to cover all the questions that could be asked. The briefing should be designed to ensure that the staff responsible for collecting intelligence are equipped with all the background information they need to carry out the project efficiently and within the time deadlines set for completion. On short assignments it is sometimes tempting to dispense with briefings. This is usually an error, largely because too much of the time available to collect intelligence is then wasted learning background information and seeking intelligence that is already available within the client department.

The topics that a typical project team briefing should cover are:

- Company background and products or services to be covered
- Reasons for requiring the intelligence
- Decisions that the intelligence is intended to support
- Key characteristics of the competitive environment
- Intelligence that is already held and known to be accurate
- Contacts
- Client actions
- Timetable

The company background and products or services to be covered

If the client is using an intelligence agency for the first time or an internal staff member that has not had previous contact with the commissioning division, the briefing should cover the company, its structure and its product ranges or services. This should include the provision of any brochures and technical literature that describe the products that are to be covered in the project.

The reasons for requiring the intelligence

The reasons for commissioning the intelligence-gathering programme should be covered in depth. This will provide the analysts with a clear idea of why they are being employed and will increase their sensitivity to intelligence that may not be in the original brief but that may prove to be available and relevant to the problem that the company is facing.

The decisions that the intelligence is intended to support

The key decisions that the company is facing should be described together with the relevance of the intelligence to those decisions. It is important to make the distinction between tactical intelligence that is required quickly to support short-term decisions and intelligence that is required on a longer-term or continuous basis to inform strategic decisions.

Key characteristics of the competitive environment (where known)

Those responsible for intelligence gathering need to be fully briefed on the nature of the competitive environment. This will help them organise the intelligence-gathering process and ensure that all relevant segments and sources of information are covered. Remember that good intelligence requires the broadest circle of contacts possible and the client briefing should be designed to ensure that as many as possible are made known to the intelligence-gathering team.

Intelligence that is already held and known to be accurate

There is no point in asking the intelligence gatherers to regenerate what is already known by the client. Rumours and suspicions about competitors should also be discussed, as long as it is made clear that they are not confirmed and should be tested. Any documentary evidence of competitors' activities in the form of reports, papers or price lists should be provided to the intelligence-gathering team. If the client is aware of any relevant exhibitions or conferences that are taking place, they should be made known to the research team. If practical the timescale for the project might need to be adjusted if particularly useful events are scheduled to take place outside the original deadlines.

Contacts

Primary intelligence requires contacts and if these are not readily available they have to be identified as part of the research process. Time can be saved and the quality of the intelligence improved if known potential sources can be identified and provided to the intelligence-gathering team. Where practical, the team should be given the opportunity to speak to any previous employees of competitors that are now employed by the commissioning company.

Client actions

Any actions to be taken by the client such as the provision of contacts or the provision of any documents need to be agreed together with the timing of their availability.

Timetable

The timetable for the assignment should be agreed together with milestone events, reporting points and meetings.

Review of Discussion Guides

A full review of the discussion guides to be used for primary intelligence gathering is usually helpful. Clients can make a valuable contribution to the questions themselves by helping to ensure that they make sense in the context of the enquiries being made and sound neither too naive nor too informed. The client should also ensure that any technical terms are correct and provide guidance on the outer limits of the responses that should be expected. This information will permit the researcher to spot unreasonable answers and challenge them in the course of the discussions.

Progress Reports

Throughout the duration of the project the client should seek regular formal and informal updates of progress. These should be designed to ensure that the project is running on time, that the data that are required are being obtained, whether modifications to the approach or the intelligence yield are required and whether there are additional contributions that the client can make to the project. Progress meetings can take the form of informal telephone contact and interim presentations at which findings are presented and discussed.

Reviews of the Information Yield

One of the key skills in primary competitive intelligence gathering is knowing when the limits have been reached and that it is time to stop. This calls for considerable frankness on both sides. Gatherers should not see a failure to obtain intelligence as a sign of weakness. Providing they have exhausted all potential sources it is preferable to admit that there is no point in proceeding further than to waste resources on seeking to obtain the unobtainable. Clients need to recognise that failures will be inevitable for a number of good reasons and that there comes a time when it is not reasonable to insist that intelligence gatherers continue to pursue sources. The benefit of frequent reporting meetings is that warning signals can be identified at the earliest practical moment and resources reallocated to more fruitful enquiries.

In addition to intelligence that is unobtainable the review process should also be structured to consider whether:

- The research findings suggest that there are additional aspects of competitors' activities or the competitive environment that require investigation
- There are additional competitors that should be covered
- Strongly held beliefs about competitors are being challenged and that additional supporting evidence will be required in order to convince management that the new information is accurate
- New competitive challenges have been identified that are outside the original framework of the assignment and will require extra effort to cover

Final Review of Findings

Once the intelligence report has been written and submitted to the client, the intelligence-gathering team should be invited to present its findings to those of the staff and management that will use the data. This makes a vital contribution to the process of selling competitive intelligence internally by permitting management to understand the results and, if necessary, challenge the methodology, the interpretation and the conclusions reached by the intelligence team.

15 Legal Factors and Ethical Guidelines

Ethics, or what is deemed to be good or bad in human conduct, is a key issue in all types of research activity. The part of competitive intelligence that focuses on the study of competitors is particularly prone to ethical assessment and is also subject to legal constraints. This is partly because there are many who regard it as an invasion of privacy, and therefore inherently unethical, and partly because there have been widely publicised situations in which the methods used to collect intelligence have been open to criticism. Competitor intelligence suffers from the fact that it is frequently compared with activities that do not adhere to the same ethical standards as other research activities and also that there are organisations that are prepared to break the law in order to acquire intelligence, if the price is right. These organisations are not part of the competitive intelligence community but are trading on the back of the growing demand for competitor intelligence.

An eminent journalist once gave a presentation on how his team obtained information for investigative reports. He stated that there were three main methods. If people wanted to see a situation exposed in the press they often volunteered information to journalists. If it was not volunteered the journalist might decide to pay for it. If it could not be obtained voluntarily or by payment the journalist might engage in some sort of subterfuge to obtain it. Given the types of assignments the team of journalists was working on, it was felt that the ends more than justified the means. The audience of competitive intelligence professionals silently wished that their task could be that easy but also wondered why the press displays such a high propensity to portray competitive intelligence as unethical.

Competitive intelligence takes place within a legal framework that has strengthened over the 1990s though not as dramatically as the legislators would have the world believe. Much of what is actionable under the new laws was already possible, though the routes were less clear and they were not aimed specifically at intelligence. Although the need to protect the assets of organisations and individuals was universally recognised, soft assets, such as information, were not regarded with the same level of seriousness as tangible objects. The dawn of the information age and the mushrooming of companies that had very few assets other than their intellectual property has changed the perception of what it is necessary to protect.

The legal and ethical issues of which competitive intelligence analysts must be aware are:

- Criminal law
- Copyright law
- Antitrust legislation
- The Economic Espionage Act
- Data protection legislation
- Industry and corporate codes of ethics

Criminal Law

Criminal law protects companies and individuals from theft, fraud and trespass. It also covers some specific activities such as phone tapping. Unfortunately the law can be difficult and expensive to use by organisations as protection for their trade secrets, except in the most blatant cases, and the penalties are often too low to provide a real deterrent. There are a number of grey areas that tempt organisations that are prepared to turn a blind eye to practices that are not strictly illegal but are clearly unethical. The classic case relates to documents that are thrown into waste bins. Obtaining them whilst they are still on the company's premises is theft and may also involve an act of trespass; retrieving them once they had left the company's premises and are therefore 'in the public domain' has been judged to be legal, though there are few that would regard it as ethical.

Copyright Law

Copyright law prevents the copying and redistribution of all written material without the permission of the author. Companies operating competitive intelligence systems are probably more likely to infringe copyright law than anything else. The 'fair use' rules state that it is possible to post extracts from published works, journals and newspapers on a corporate competitive intelligence system but posting complete articles is an infringement of copyright. On-line vendors of information, such as Dialog or Reuters, normally restrict their customers' rights to copy, store or sell the information that they provide, in its original format. Copyright law also protects information on competitors' websites.

There are two options for those wishing to use published information. If it is required in its original format it is possible to buy a licence that permits the use of articles in their original format. If this is not required, copyright law does not apply to information that has been reworked into an analysis, which is what most analysts require it for.

Competition and Antitrust Legislation

In Europe and the United States all in-house staff gathering competitive intelligence must take care that their activities cannot be interpreted as being anti-competitive. In particular, exchanges of information on pricing, discounting and marketing practices can easily fall foul of antitrust and competition legislation by suggesting either collusion between suppliers or the formation of an illegal cartel. It is worth noting that the Office of Fair Trading in the United Kingdom and its equivalents elsewhere are quite vigilant in their searches for anti-competitive activity and keen to prosecute when they feel they can prove that companies have infringed competition law.

The Economic Espionage Act

In the United States, any analyst tempted to step outside the ethical code that governs their activities must consider the Economic Espionage and Protection of Proprietary Information Act. Enacted in 1996 this makes it a Federal criminal offence to carry out certain actions that are designed to obtain the intellectual property of another organisation. The Act specifies that it is an offense to steal, take or defraud another of a 'trade secret' relating to a product or service that has been produced by or placed in interstate or foreign commerce, for the economic benefit of someone other than the owner or for the benefit of a foreign government. 'Trade secrets' are defined as all kinds of financial, business, scientific, technical, economic or engineering information that their owners have taken reasonable measures to keep secret and which have independent economic value because they are not generally known to the public and are not readily known through proper means.

Clearly the Act provides no protection for information that can be identified by what it calls 'proper means' or which the owner has not taken 'reasonable steps' to protect. But it is also clear that the types of activity that are generally understood as being 'espionage' are likely to fall well within the bounds of the Act as could extremely aggressive and deceitful primary data collection.

Misappropriation of trade secrets is also covered by individual State laws that have adopted either the Restatement of Torts (1939) or the Uniform Trade Secrets Act. This gives the owner of a trade secret the right to sue for damages if they can show that it has been acquired by improper methods. Improper is defined as taking it without the owner's permission when reasonable steps had been taken to protect it.

In addition to the specific Acts relating to trade secrets there are a variety of other legal traps that the unwary collector of intelligence can fall foul of if the data collection procedures can be shown to be unreasonable. These include Unfair Trade or Business Practices and Unjust Enrichment.[1]

Data Protection Legislation

European countries do not have the equivalent of an Economic Espionage Act and rely on the broader protection provided by laws protecting companies from theft, fraud, bribery, trespass and illegal phone tapping. However, they have enacted legislation that has a more directly restrictive effect on competitive intelligence in the form of data protection legislation. In 1995 the European Union adopted the European Data Protection Directive that required all member countries to enact data protection legislation. This was designed to protect the privacy of individuals by controlling the content and use of databases containing personal information. This wording might suggest that it affects only large electronic databases but in practice the definition covers any compilation of personal information about an individual that is stored – however small. Although this may seem absurd and unenforceable, it has to be taken into account when profiling the management of competitive companies. Given the importance of individual managers in determining the actions of competitors and the consequent need to know who they are and how they work, data protection legislation strikes at the heart of competitor intelligence.

The United Kingdom version of the legislation is enshrined in the Data Protection Act enacted in March 2000. The requirements are being introduced gradually over the period 2000 to 2007. The Act states that in order to process personal information one of six possible conditions must be fulfilled. These are that the data are being used:

• With the consent of the individual being studied
• In the performance of a contract
• To comply with legal obligations
• To protect the vital interests of the individual being studied
• For the administration of justice
• As a necessary component of legitimate interests

Some of these conditions seem very general and open to an interpretation that permits personal profiling for competitive intelligence. However, it is unlikely that a competitive intelligence assignment would be regarded as being a legitimate interest, certainly when viewed from the perspective of the subject.

Although purely European the legislation affects the activities of analysts based in the United States through a privacy pact negotiated between the European Union and the United States. This requires US companies to abide by European rules when dealing with data on European individuals.

The United Kingdom data protection legislation is policed by a Commissioner for Data Protection who has the power to investigate possible infringements and institute proceedings. Similar arrangements apply in other European countries that have complied with the European Directive.[2]

Codes of Ethics

Members of the Society for Competitive Intelligence Professionals are required to abide by a Code of Ethics that provides a measure of protection for their information sources, themselves and the companies they work for. The most important consideration in the Code is the protection of information sources, since it is they that stand to be damaged most in the event of any unacceptable practices. The requirements the Code places on professionals are:

- To continually strive to increase respect and recognition for the profession
- To pursue one's duties with zeal and diligence while maintaining the highest degree of professionalism and avoiding unethical practices
- To faithfully adhere to and abide by one's company policies, objectives and guidelines
- To comply with all applicable laws
- To accurately disclose all relevant information, including one's identity and organisation, prior to all interviews
- To fully respect all requests for confidentiality of information
- To promote and encourage full compliance with these ethical standards within one's company, with third party contractors, and within the entire profession

A cynic might say that the details of the Code are in the eye of the beholder and that it leaves the door wide open for very liberal interpretation. However, it does specifically exclude everything that is illegal and any act of misrepresentation.

Most large companies have developed codes of business ethics for their employees. Whilst these do not normally cover competitive intelligence specifically some companies that make heavy use of competitive intelligence have incorporated guidelines that they require their staff and any contractors working on their behalf to adhere to. These tend to be substantially more restrictive and far more detailed than the SCIP Code and are clearly designed to ensure that there is no chance that their competitive intelligence activities will result in a court action or, as is more likely, bad publicity.

Non-Disclosure

Competitive intelligence tends to be central to the strategies of those companies using it and in order to provide actionable intelligence it is often necessary to know highly sensitive information about the user company. When it is necessary to provide such information to outsiders in order to enable them to fulfil intelligence-gathering contracts it is normal to require them to sign non-disclosure agreements that are binding on any individual working on the contract. This provides a measure of protection that the clients' trade secrets will not be passed on to third parties. It is clearly in the interest of agencies to ensure that such agreements are taken seriously and that all possible steps are taken to ensure that no client information leaks out of their organisations. This implies that agencies should operate secure working environments in which:

- The staff that are employed are discreet and honest
- Sensitive documents are accessible only to those staff that have a need to see them
- When not in use documents are stored in secure cabinets
- Access to the premises is controlled
- All client documents are returned to clients on completion of the contract
- Staff leaving the company are asked to provide an undertaking that they will not disclose client secrets that they have been party to

Conflicts of Interest

Agencies providing competitive intelligence must exercise great care when working for clients that compete in the same business. By the same token clients need to be careful when selecting agencies, to be sure that there is no risk that data that are client-confidential will be passed, even inadvertently, to a competitor. The risk is greatest when using agencies that specialise in a business sector, commonly the case in pharmaceuticals and telecommunications. There are nevertheless distinct advantages in working with agencies that know the business well and in many cases these may override the fear that there could be a conflict of interest.

The ultimate protection is for agencies to volunteer to work exclusively for a single client in the sector or a specific segment within the sector. Clients may also request an undertaking that the agency does not work for a named list of competitors within a reasonable time-frame.

Market Research and Competitive Intelligence Ethics

The ethics for competitive intelligence and market research have much in common but differ in some key respects. The market research business requires that practitioners protect the interests of respondents by:

- Providing a full disclosure of information relating to the purpose of the survey and the uses to which the data will be put before any interviews are carried out
- Maintaining respondents' freedom to participate in a research exercise or not
- Establishing the bona fides of the research agency
- Protecting the identity of respondents
- Not disclosing information provided by specific respondents
- Protecting respondents from sales approaches based on the data they provide

The respondent is the most valuable asset that the research business has and anything which reduces respondents' willingness to cooperate in future surveys is not only unfortunate for the respondents but will also undermine the ability of researchers to collect information. In practice only a small proportion of the population have ever participated in research programmes but there is a much higher level of awareness of research and if awareness is accompanied by adverse opinion it can be a powerful disincentive to cooperate.

In a competitive intelligence enquiry some of the above constraints apply but given the purpose of the investigation some are clearly unworkable. When dealing with primary intelligence sources it is not feasible to tell respondents the full purpose of the enquiry. Were this to be done, no intelligence would be obtained. Respondents are protected in that there is no misrepresentation but not to the extent that there is full disclosure. All respondents have the freedom to participate or not depending on whether they feel it is in their interest to do so and this may be based in part on the credentials of the individual or agency carrying out the investigation.

The identity of respondents certainly can be protected and it is not essential to make a link between data provided and the individual providing it. It should be possible to demonstrate that the sources used are qualified to provide the intelligence without going so far as to state who said what. Nevertheless, in competitive intelligence it is common to provide a list of intelligence sources, by job title if not by name.

The key difference between competitive intelligence and market research is that whereas in research information about individual respondents is rarely useful, in competitive intelligence information about employees and the companies that employ a high proportion of the respondents is the sole purpose of the enquiry.

A question that is rarely asked but is occasionally relevant is what happens if, within a wholly ethical research approach, a respondent discloses intelligence that they obviously should not have revealed and, if used, could have a serious adverse effect on the future performance of the company being investigated. One school of thought takes the view that all is fair in love and war and whatever a respondent can be tempted to disclose automatically enters the public domain and can be used. The other admits that the respondent has made an error of judgement and suppresses the intelligence. Opinion may differ according to whether the observer is a source or a recipient of intelligence but many users state clearly that intelligence obtained under those circumstances will not be accepted. A similar debate surrounds intelligence that is 'found' in discarded waste, from documents mislaid in public places or from laptops that are lost.

Deliverables

Agencies and in-house competitor analysts have a responsibility to deliver the research programme that the client company or client department has paid for. Unless alterations in methodology and coverage are agreed in advance with the client, the number and type of interviews, the content of the investigation and the depth and quality of the analysis should be as set out in the research proposal. If there are deviations these should be agreed with the client, they should be explained and their impact on the results should be stated. The report that is delivered to the client must be a fair representation of what was found. Spurious levels of accuracy must not be claimed and, where relevant, the levels of confidence in the data should be stated. If for any reason the investigation failed to work or did not yield the quality of results that were expected, this should be admitted and a course of corrective action agreed.

Sanctions

Although the sanctions for breaking the law can be severe, unethical behaviour does not necessarily result in any significant penalties. Furthermore if ethical codes are not strictly enforced they may be forgotten or ignored because the chances of being caught out are remote. In practice, the worst sanctions that can be incurred from unethical intelligence collection are the adverse publicity that can result from public exposure and a possible loss of trust from customers. The latter could offset any gains in profit that might result from using the intelligence.

Regional Variations

Rather like beauty, ethics are in the eye of the beholder. Taken at a global level, what is clearly unacceptable from an ethical standpoint in some countries is regarded as normal practice in others. In large parts of the world paying for information, for business and for political favours in cash or kind is regarded as a perfectly normal business practice but is not acceptable in Europe or North America. Some governments permit their security services to collect commercial intelligence, which they then disseminate to companies; others regard this as an unethical use of publicly funded resources. The dilemma this creates for multinational companies is whether they should apply a global standard for all their operations or whether they should work to local standards. Whilst there is undoubtedly a problem in persuading local staff to fight local battles with one arm tied behind their back there is an even greater problem if local practices are exposed internationally and used to demonstrate that a global company is behaving unethically. Whatever explanation is given, it never sounds convincing to audiences that have never worked outside Europe or North America.

Notes

1. These and the Economic Espionage Act are described in detail by William Duffey Jr, 'Competitive Information Collection: Avoiding Legal Landmines', *Competitive Intelligence Review*, vol. 11, no. 3, Third Quarter 2000, pp. 37–53.
2. Chris Brogan has written extensively about European data protection legislation. See John McGonagle and Chris Brogan, 'The EU Directive and the British Data Protection Act – A Transatlantic Conversation', *Competitive Intelligence Magazine*, vol. 3, no. 4, October–December 2000, pp. 45–8.

16 Processing and Distributing Intelligence

One of the key tasks of competitive intelligence analysts is to ensure that their findings reach the staff that can use them within an acceptable time-frame. This may sound obvious but is worth stating, first, because a high proportion of intelligence is useful only for a short period of time and, second, because staff that collect competitive intelligence tend to be more security-conscious than most and have a tendency to keep the most useful data to themselves.

The demand for competitive intelligence evolved long before the development of computerised communication systems. This meant that most intelligence changed hands manually in the form of written documents. Written reports are still used in a high proportion of companies, though now they may be e-mailed rather than physically copied. However, the advent of efficient and secure internal communication systems means that there are ready mechanisms for collecting intelligence from internal sources, for verifying it and for ensuring that it is distributed quickly to the staff that can use it. Systems can also be used by staff to notify the analysts of their competitive intelligence requirements.

A common problem faced by all internal competitive intelligence analysts is generating sufficient enthusiasm about their programmes to persuade executives to spend time contributing information and studying the results on a regular basis. Although they have no problem gaining attention at times of intense competitive activity, the enthusiasm for competitive intelligence tends to evaporate once the crisis has passed. The threats posed by competitors are ever present and unless staff continuously update their knowledge and act on the basis of small signals, what starts as a minor threat can soon escalate into a crisis. This means that there is a considerable premium to be placed on delivering intelligence by means that gain the attention of its potential users and minimise the amount of time they need to spend assimilating it.

The processing and distribution options that are available are:

- The distribution of written reports
- Meetings and forums in which competitive intelligence is presented and discussed
- E-mail
- Corporate intranets
- Management (or marketing) information systems
- Knowledge management systems
- Tailored competitive intelligence systems

The choice will depend on the size of the organisation, the importance attached to the use of competitive intelligence and the budget that is available.

Written Reports

In medium and small companies the written report remains the most cost-effective method of distributing competitive intelligence. Manual systems are cumbersome and carry the risk of finding their way into the wrong hands but are more user-friendly to the majority that still prefer to absorb data off a page rather than a screen and at times and in places where screens are not available. The attraction of the printed page is amply demonstrated by the high proportion of electronically distributed documents that are printed before being read.

Meetings and Other Forums

Meetings and other methods that bring executives together are rarely time-saving but are more likely to gain attention than intelligence reports. They also have the advantage that they can be organised at times that do not eat into the working day, such as breakfast or lunch meetings with a modest bribe in the form of refreshments!

The value of competitive intelligence is considerably enhanced when staff using intelligence have the opportunity to discuss it with those that collect it. The personal interface permits users to describe their requirements in detail and, after the data have been obtained, to ask questions. Meetings between staff are the most common method of interacting but internal seminars, workshops and exhibitions are also being used with considerable success. Seminars and workshops at which intelligence is presented formally and then discussed bring the benefit of collective working. This is further enhanced in the case of workshops in which intelligence is used as the basis for developing solutions to specific competitive problems.

Exhibitions have been used with some success to display material on groups of competitors. Each 'stand' at the exhibition covers a single competitor and is manned by staff that have studied the company. The material on display can comprise profiles of competitor companies, examples of products, marketing materials, profiles of the key management and deductions about their strategies.

E-mail

E-mail has the major advantage of gaining instant attention from recipients. It is therefore an ideal medium for distributing competitive newsletters or 'alerts' containing information that needs to be acted upon quickly.

Corporate Intranets

Intranets, the internal equivalent of the Internet, are rapidly gaining acceptance as a vehicle for collecting and sharing information within organisations. They have the advantages of simplicity and ease of use, but are more difficult to tailor to competitive intelligence purposes than database management systems. Furthermore, the intranet is a passive participant in the knowledge management process. It connects information gatherers with information users but does not in itself overcome the cultural problems that act as a barrier to information exchange. Nor can it filter or manipulate information unless special software packages are installed on it.

Security is a serious issue with intranets and competitive intelligence reports posted on them should be at least password-protected in order to limit access to those authorised to read them.

Management Information Systems

Management, or, more specifically, marketing information systems, have been in existence for some time and can certainly incorporate competitive intelligence. To be fully effective an information system must be something more than a passive store of information. It also needs to be dynamic in the sense that it:

- Stimulates the flow of information to users
- Triggers the actions required to fill information gaps
- Ensures that the information available from the system is continuously updated to meet the changing needs of the organisation

This suggests a system that is an important component of the working environment of the various departments that use it and that is used continuously. It also suggests that they are electronic though a number of manual systems are still in existence.

The key functions of a management information system are:

- To act as a repository for all intelligence that is relevant to the company's management, including data generated internally from the company's own records, data collected regularly from key secondary sources, data that have been purchased or commissioned from external sources and anecdotal information on customers, distributors and competitors collected by the sales force and others having regular external contacts
- To ensure that the intelligence which is used continuously is always up to date
- To sift and interpret incoming information, determine its accuracy and grade its importance to the company's current and future operations
- To identify intelligence gaps either by matching information needs with information available on the system or by processing intelligence requests from line managers
- To distribute data that have been acquired and alert management to significant developments, threats and opportunities

By bringing together all of the intelligence that a company collects from internal and external sources and by means of secondary and primary research, an effective management information system can not only improve information utilisation but can also save money. Regardless of the purpose for which the information was collected, it can often be recycled for other applications. Furthermore, large organisations can duplicate intelligence-collection costs as different departments specify the same needs and either commission their own exercises or purchase the same published reports.

To be useful, and to encourage staff to use it, a management information system must contain most (if not all) of the intelligence that managers require on a regular basis. Whilst managers will accept that exceptional or unusual intelligence needs are not catered for by the system and therefore have to be resourced separately, they will soon run out of patience with a system that fails to answer routine questions. The definition of what constitutes routine intelligence will vary from company to company but generally includes current news, the latest financial information, products and services offered, management changes, prices, market segments serviced and key customers.

A system can also contain a facility for staff to enter information and interpretations of their own, to make comments on data or trends for others in the company to consider and to request additional intelligence. Security systems need to be in place to prevent intelligence being overwritten or lost and, more importantly, to prevent unauthorised access.

Whilst there is no physical limit, other than storage space, to what is placed on a management information system, the system must be easy to navigate and users must be able to locate and retrieve the information they require quickly. Large systems need not be cumbersome but they must be well-designed to make them user-friendly. Some of the standard software packages which have been developed to handle large-scale information systems are notoriously difficult to operate and may require considerable modification.

Like all databases, a management information system requires constant updating. In the case of competitive intelligence this can be daily. Data inputs can come from a wide variety of sources within and outside the company and the management of the system and control over what is placed on it needs to be the responsibility of one person (or team of people). The primary management task is to ensure that what is placed on the system is relevant to the company's business, accurate and timely. Without proper stewardship the database will either atrophy and fall into disuse or will become so overloaded with irrelevant data, fed in by enthusiastic but uninformed staff, that it will become impossible to use efficiently.

In the case of competitor information using electronic newsfeeds can facilitate the task of inputting news items. Similarly all customised reports on competitors should be received in electronic format so that they can be entered directly without retranscription.

Knowledge Management Systems

Knowledge management systems and the older management information systems have much in common but differ in one key respect. A management information system is, as its name implies, solely concerned with the storage and processing of information whereas a knowledge management system incorporates systems that assist its users to elevate information to knowledge and then store and disseminate the resultant output. Knowledge management systems are replacing management information systems and knowledge managers are beginning to supplant information officers.

The problem of integrating knowledge into the decision-making processes of a company is not unique to competitive strategy development. Most other corporate functions use information that needs to be collected, processed, interpreted and distributed and there can be considerable overlap in the information needs of departments. For example, competitive intelligence is directly relevant to the sales and marketing department but may also be important to corporate strategy, production and human resources, particularly if it contains benchmarking data. Knowledge management is a new discipline that encompasses the total information needs of a company obtained from internal and external sources. It feeds into all business processes and integrates hard data with 'soft' assets of an organisation, namely the creative contributions that can be made by staff.

A key difference from traditional information systems is that knowledge management acknowledges the importance not only of *explicit knowledge* – that which is written down and incorporated in inventories – but also *tacit knowledge* – the understanding that individual staff members carry around in their heads or in their personal records. Within the marketing function, for example, sales representatives are a major repository of information that is rarely acknowledged, let alone brought together. Even though it may be subject to all sorts of distortions and biases, it can provide considerable insight into the status and development of a market and the competitors active within it. The focus of the picture of the market that is provided may be considerably sharpened when data from all sales representatives are compared and rationalised.

The system improves efficiency by increasing the availability and use of the information assets that the company has acquired by:

● Tapping the data collection and creative resources of all relevant staff in the organisation

- Minimising the chances of the same tasks being repeated in separate parts of the organisation
- Making a consensus interpretation available to all
- Maintaining the currency of the information

Knowledge management systems are usually associated with powerful database management systems, such as Lotus Notes, which are capable of handling large volumes of data. The hardware and software are indeed a valuable component, especially in large organisations, but are not essential to the process. The primary task is to gain acceptance that knowledge is required throughout the organisation and that it can be created and distributed if all of the relevant staff have access to raw data and can work on them for their own purposes and for the common benefit of the system. This can be achieved manually without the burden of designing an automated system. Indeed, it is advisable to establish a manual system and prove that it works and is accepted before major investments are made in hardware and software.

Nevertheless a growing number of custom-designed knowledge management systems are being developed and made available to organisations that embrace the concept. Some typical systems are described below and have been selected to show how knowledge management differs fundamentally from more traditional methods of sharing information within organisations.

Knowledgex (http://www.knowledgex.com)

This is a software application for acquiring, discovering, publishing and distributing knowledge across an organisation. It aims to tap into employees' knowledge about a market, to share this information with people who need to know and develop a knowledge base with a simple-to-use visual interface.

6DOS (http://www.6dos.com)

This system offers connecting, tracking and rewarding facilities. The connecting facility provides a question-and-answer system to help reach those individuals within an organisation who will know the answers to questions. The tracking function follows through the flow of information of questions and answers to create an archive for re-use. The rewarding function encourages people in the organisation to participate by providing incentives.

Wisewire (http://www.wisewire.com)

Wisewire is held on an organisation's website or intranet. It feeds in real-time information or delivers personalised profiles to interested parties. The content comprises on-line sources, premium sources, newsgroups, mailing lists and the organisation's own proprietary information. The most relevant information can be archived to provide a searchable resource.

Intraspect (http://www.intraspect.com)

Intraspect enables the collection, organisation and re-use of information via a single interface. The contents of the organisation's memory are indexed to enable filtered and focused searching. The search results show the contexts of the returned documents so the user can easily see what parts of the organisation are relevant. Comments can be attached to documents and discussion groups set up through the interface or by e-mail.

Tailored Competitive Intelligence Systems

Analysts can use any of the large number of standard packages that have been developed for database management, data filtering, data mining and text retrieval in order to access, organise, store, manage and distribute competitive intelligence. Where they have already been installed as part of an overall management information system they probably represent the most cost-effective solution for competitive intelligence, even though they may require adaptation to maximise their usefulness. In the absence of an existing commitment, competitive intelligence analysts can consider investing in a tailor-made competitive intelligence system. Typically these are based on database management and groupware systems, such as Lotus Notes, and a corporate intranet. The attraction of these systems is that the work of adapting the standard systems to meet the specific requirements of competitive intelligence has already been carried out and they can be installed on a turnkey basis.

Tailor-made competitive intelligence systems bear a strong resemblance to the management information and knowledge management systems described above.[1] The differences are in the detailed features that have been inserted for competitive intelligence purposes rather than in the overall concept. Indeed, suppliers of competitive intelligence systems see themselves as being members of the broader knowledge management community.

Although there are companies that prefer to have a separate competitive intelligence system rather than a management information system that contains competitive intelligence, tailored systems are a costly investment and are not necessarily the best method of starting a competitive intelligence function. Their justification lies in the fact that they can save considerable set-up time and also import the expertise that their developers have gained over many years in the competitive intelligence business.

A typical competitive intelligence system will carry out the following functions:

- Database – hold an indexed and searchable database comprising internal and externally generated material from diverse sources in text, graphic, HTML, voice and video formats
- Inputs – permits staff to input intelligence and comments whenever they review material held on the database; this meets the need to engage as many staff as possible in the intelligence collection and appraisal processes
- Tasking – requesting individuals throughout the company to carry out tasks that result in intelligence being created and then monitoring their activities
- Analysis – organising and sorting complex sets of data in response to specific problems in order to facilitate the achievement of a solution
- Reports – using the database to create reports on topics as they arise
- Communications – sharing the data and analysis that have been created with all those who are mandated to use them

The content of these systems is updated continuously by automatic data feeds and by the manual insertion of data.

Access to Competitive Intelligence

Competitive intelligence needs to be accessed by all staff involved in the development of corporate strategy by senior marketing management, by market planners and by certain line marketing staff such as brand and product managers, sales staff and specialists such as advertising and PR.

In the security world intelligence systems are defined as being either 'open' or 'closed'. In a closed system all of the content is classified as secret and only those that have a 'need to know' can have access to it. 'Need' can be defined in a highly restrictive manner and access can be limited to very few people. It is evident that the unlimited access to an 'open' system poses security risks, which could be avoided by removing temptation, but it is equally clear that if access to competitive intelligence is too restricted it will not gain the widespread use that is required to justify the cost of collecting it.

Most competitive intelligence systems limit access to:

- Those who can contribute to the database either by inputting facts or commentary
- Those who have the ability to use the output from the database

This does not include all staff and minimises the risk of staff passing intelligence contained on the system out to third parties, either deliberately or inadvertently.

The conflicting demands of maintaining overall security whilst at the same time ensuring that intelligence reaches all of those that can make use of it can be overcome by manual intervention. 'Need to know' does not mean need to know everything that is on the competitive intelligence system any more than the existence of a system will ensure that those that need to consult it will actually do so. Some of the most prolific and effective users of competitive intelligence rely on their internal analysts to distribute manually specific items of intelligence to those they feel can use it, together with an interpretation of what they feel it could mean to the recipient. This process can be far more effective in stimulating a dialogue between intelligence gatherer and intelligence user than any system can achieve on its own.

Note

1. In a 2001 survey of competitive intelligence software systems Leonard Fuld of Fuld & Company covered the following twelve systems: C-4-U Scout (C-4-U Ltd.), Competitive Intelligence Spider (Knowledge Computing Corp.), Knowledge Works (Cipher Systems), Market Signal Analyzer (Docere Intelligence), E-Sense (Vigil Technologies), Corporate Intelligence Service (Intelliseek Inc.), TextAnalyst (Megaputer Intelligence Inc.), Plumtree Corporate Portal (Plumtree Software Inc.), Powerize.com (Powerize.com), Strategy (Strategy Software Inc.), Wincite (Wincite Systems LLC), Wisdom Builder (Wisdombuilder LLC).

17 Measuring the Effectiveness of Competitive Intelligence

The effectiveness of all business processes and activities should be measured and competitive intelligence is no exception, especially since it is an activity that can absorb a considerable budget. Even if companies do not feel a need to demonstrate that they are spending their money wisely, competitive intelligence managers should be interested in proving that they are making a contribution to performance, if only to create some measure of protection when the next round of redundancies is being considered.

Unfortunately it is rarely possible to detect a direct correlation between the use of competitive intelligence and company performance. Management therefore has to rely on a series of separate indicators in order to determine whether the investment in competitive intelligence is worthwhile. Most of the indicators are qualitative though in some instances it is possible to use quantitative measures.

The five key indicators of the effectiveness of competitive intelligence are:

- Quality of intelligence provided
- Use being made of competitive intelligence
- Development of an intelligence culture
- Event analysis
- Market share

Quality of Intelligence Provided

In order to be effective, competitive intelligence must be of sufficient depth and quality to make a contribution to decisions and must also be sufficiently timely to eliminate surprises. Reviewing the output of the competitive intelligence department can test all of these. The key questions that should be asked regularly are:

- Accuracy – does the intelligence normally prove to be accurate?
- Depth – is the intelligence provided sufficiently detailed to facilitate the definition of counter measures?
- Relevance – does the intelligence cover topics that are relevant to the day-to-day management of our business?
- Responsiveness – when special requests are made does the system provide a response within an acceptable timescale?
- Timing – is the intelligence received with sufficient lead-time for the company to make effective plans?
- Comprehensiveness – how frequently do events occur that were not flagged in advance by the competitive intelligence system? How frequently are we taken by surprise?

Use Being Made of Competitive Intelligence

The primary indicator of whether competitive intelligence is working for an organisation is the extent to which it is being used and the build-up of demand for intelligence. Use does not necessarily mean effectiveness but if staff are demanding increasing amounts of intelligence as part of the process by which they make decisions and formulate their plans, it is reasonable to assume that they feel it is making a contribution.

This assumption can be made more tangible by asking users to pay for intelligence. Many competitive intelligence departments have been set up as profit rather than cost centres and cross-charge for their services. As willingness to spend money on a service normally means that it is thought to be making a contribution, growth in the demand placed on a competitive intelligence department that charges for its services suggests that its output is working.

A further refinement of the assessment is the extent to which demand is sustained through periods of recession. There are examples of competitive intelligence departments that have been established and heavily promoted internally and that have built up a loyal group of users within the company. At first the demand may be driven by the novelty of the service as much as by its usefulness. However, at the first sign of problems and a reduction in departmental budgets, intelligence of all types can be an early casualty. This level of dispensability suggests a service that is regarded as being peripheral to performance rather than essential. If this happens it is an extremely harsh judgement on the perceived effectiveness of competitive intelligence. It is much easier to ignore competitors when markets are growing. Competition strengthens in times of recession and this is the very time when the intelligence can make its most valuable contribution.

Development of an Intelligence Culture

The third indicator of the effectiveness of competitive intelligence is the extent to which an intelligence culture builds up within a company. A strong intelligence culture is one in which:

- Large numbers of staff contribute intelligence on competitors and business trends to their corporate system
- Intelligence is always demanded before decisions are made at all levels of the company
- Staff who are not permitted access to intelligence make strong representations in order to gain access
- Victories over competitors are strongly celebrated

The acid test is whether a proposed withdrawal of the system or service would produce howls of rage or a whimper.

Event Analysis

Although it is difficult, if not impossible, to take an overall view of the contribution of competitive intelligence, at a tactical level an analysis of orders won and lost can show whether the availability of intelligence contributed to the wins and a lack of intelligence contributed to the losses. This demands a certain amount of openness on the part of sales teams, who might prefer to attribute successes to their personal capabilities and failures than to things happening elsewhere in the company, but when the analysis is brought down to each individual skirmish the role of intelligence is usually evident. This works in a negative as well as a positive sense. A lack of intelligence that would have helped win a sale is simple to determine. How often is the statement 'if only I had known ...' made? Evidence of how intelligence would have worked had it been available is just as powerful a justification as evidence of successes. Indeed one of the main triggers to the establishment of a competitive intelligence function is a major loss that has been incurred by being taken unawares by competitive action.

Market Share

The ultimate expression of successful competitive action is growth in market share. Although this can never be attributed entirely to better knowledge of the competitive environment, companies that make active use of competitive intelligence and achieve sustained growth in their market share can normally see some connection. Unfortunately, it is equally possible for users of competitive intelligence to lose market share!

18

Counter-Intelligence

PricewaterhouseCoopers have estimated that in 1999 the theft of proprietary information cost Fortune 1000 companies $45 billion.[1] The losses caused by successful competitive intelligence could be many times this figure since competitive intelligence is much more widely practised than theft. Counter-intelligence programmes represent a partial but essential defence against competitive intelligence and they should not be confused with counter-espionage. The civilian version of counter-espionage is used to counter the threat to businesses arising from:

- Industrial espionage using conventional and electronic techniques
- Bribery of staff
- Extortion
- Kidnapping of key executives
- Sabotage

Counter-espionage uses physical and electronic methods and is every bit as rough and ready as the espionage it seeks to prevent. Counter-intelligence is altogether subtler and has to be capable of dealing with intrusions that are neither illegal nor unethical. Whilst it can use barriers to prevent an exodus of information, they must be placed in company procedures and in the minds of staff, not across the entry points to sites.

In most companies responsibility for preventing the loss of secret or sensitive information is in the hands of corporate security. These departments play a policing role and are often staffed by ex-policemen. The most common security role is to control access and thereby prevent incursions by those who do not have a legitimate purpose on the company's sites. They are most closely associated with gate guarding, perimeter surveillance, logging of visitors on and off the sites and night patrols, all of which are designed to prevent the theft of equipment and documents. If security does develop a wider mandate, it is normally into the realms of counter-espionage and not counter-intelligence.

The adoption of procedures to counter competitive intelligence is in its infancy. The need for specific programmes to vet the information flowing out of the company, to prevent information leaks by stopping staff overstepping the mark when talking to third parties and to control the outflow of sensitive information from third parties associated with the company is barely recognised. This is particularly true in companies who themselves make no significant use of competitive intelligence.

It is also true, and therefore one of the key differences between counter-espionage and counter-intelligence (as defined for this book), that counter-espionage cannot afford to fail. In the world of espionage, failure spells disaster. A failure to control competitive intelligence activities may have serious consequences but is rarely elevated to the realms of being a disaster. Those countering competitive intelligence generally recognise that it is impossible to eliminate the outflow of information from their companies and counter-intelligence programmes are not designed to do so. Their objective is to restrict information outflows to that which is essential for them to trade effectively, to protect information until it is too late for competitors to use it effectively and, just possibly, to confuse competitors by using misinformation programmes.

To a very significant extent the vulnerabilities in any organisation lie in the channels through which information can pass to the outside world. Counter-intelligence therefore focuses not on information but on the channels that competitors can exploit in order to profile their organisation's activities.

The value of counter-intelligence programmes is not restricted to defence. Counter-intelligence activities themselves provide useful competitive intelligence. In addition to providing an early warning of a competitive attack, knowledge that a competitor is targeting the organisation and the types of information they are seeking may also provide an indication of:

- The source of the attack
- The subject of the attack (for example, product categories or distribution channels)
- The purpose of the attack
- The scale of the attack (if a substantial exercise is being carried out this suggests that it is being used to underpin major competitive action)
- The timing of the attack

Counter-intelligence can therefore make an important contribution to the counter-attack, which should be the inevitable response to any competitive action.

The Structure of Counter-Intelligence Activity

Like any other serious business activity, counter-intelligence should be formally structured, resourced and provided with an 'activity champion' or team. Informal activity is unlikely to be effective nor is it likely to be applied consistently. Whilst it is true that serious intelligence breaches will result in a heightened sensitivity to the need to prevent information passing out of the company, this does not usually last long unless programmes are in place to ensure that vigilance is maintained.

The Basic Steps

Counter-intelligence can be constructed as a nine-step programme as set out below. The requirement for each step and the amount of resources allocated to it depend on the nature and scale of the competitive intelligence programmes that are being mounted and the subject companies' interpretation of what is at risk.

- Assign responsibility for counter-intelligence programmes
- Identify the potential sources of competitive intelligence threats
- Identify the means by which the intelligence can be sought
- Identify and assess the vulnerabilities
- Categorise information
- Reduce the chances of intelligence being obtained
- Test the counter-intelligence system
- Monitor the threat
- Publicise willingness to take action

Assigning Responsibility for Counter-Intelligence Programmes

For most companies it is reasonable to assume that at some stage they will be the target of an intelligence-gathering programme. Some companies, typically the largest, the most innovative, those using or producing the most advanced technology, those occupying market leadership positions, the most profitable and those growing the fastest should always assume that one or more of their competitors is seeking information on their activities. However, the intensity of the attack will vary over time and it is always useful to know when intelligence-gathering activity is gathering pace. Any intensification of information-collection activity may provide early warning of a competitive attack and may also suggest that the company is treading on some delicate toes in the marketplace and forcing them into retaliatory action.

Whilst an assumption of intelligence activity may be reasonable, it is not always possible to determine that an intelligence-gathering exercise is actually being carried out. Some attacks leave no trace. For example, when data are being collected by methods that require no contact with the company or its close affiliates, there is no mechanism that will automatically alert the company to the fact that intelligence is being collected. Furthermore, not all direct enquiries are easy to link to intelligence-gathering. For example, enquiries by seemingly genuine customers will not normally be regarded as suspicious, unless there is an obvious incompatibility between the enquirer and the information being requested.

The key organisational aspects of counter-intelligence are:

- The fact that competitive intelligence can be extremely difficult to detect means that counter-intelligence operations must be consciously organised if they are going to be in any way effective
- Counter-intelligence programmes must be in place and working continuously regardless of whether a competitive attack is under way or not.
- The nature of a competitive intelligence attack means that the whole company must be involved in the counter-intelligence programme. The only safe assumption is that all employees are likely to be targeted as sources of intelligence and all of them must therefore be made aware of the fact and made party to the counter-intelligence programme

In order to meet these objectives it is necessary to assign responsibility for counter-intelligence and to establish an alert system into which all information relating to possible competitive intelligence activities is fed. This can be a manual system or a software solution designed to capture relevant information, analyse it and search for patterns of activity. Responsibility for counter-intelligence can be assigned in various ways, depending on the likely scale of the threat, the amount of damage that an information leak could inflict and the resources that are available, but there is no simple or obvious method of coping with the problem. The options to be considered are:

- Recruit a counter-intelligence specialist to coordinate the programme. This is the best but most difficult option to implement, since few such specialists exist. The next-best option is to train a recruit into the job
- Broaden the mandate of the head of security beyond the responsibility for physical security. This is an option but depends on the character of the incumbent and their ability to handle the subtleties of counter-intelligence in addition to the more physical (and sometimes more pressing) demands of access control and general policing activities. Whilst the ex-police and military personnel commonly used for security are generally able to recognise an intruder, they do not normally have the right temperament or experience to deal with the multiplicity of methods by which information can leak out of an organisation
- Assign responsibility to an existing staff member who is close to intelligence-gathering operations, possibly the head of competitive or business intelligence. This approach is not ideal since their existing roles are already likely to be quite demanding. However, it would ensure that counter-intelligence becomes integrated with the competitive and business intelligence-gathering processes and therefore that the threats exposed by counter-intelligence programmes are fed into the competitive strategy and acted on
- Assign responsibility to the staff member responsible for controlling the dissemination of information about the company, such as the Director of Public Affairs. This is an option but good PR staff are better at getting messages across to the various 'publics' they need to address than restricting the outflows of information

Once recruited, the tasks of the head of the counter-intelligence operation would need to be all-embracing if effectiveness were to be assured. These would include the following:

- Ensure that all written documents passing out of the company are vetted in order to ascertain that they do not contain details which are unnecessarily revealing or data which would permit external analysts to deduce the plans and strategies of the company. The vetting process can be delegated to those in a position to determine whether the information contained in documents and websites is too explicit. The most useful staff in this context are:
  - Competitive intelligence analysts
  - Business intelligence staff
  - Strategic planners
  - Marketing planners

  all of whom are likely to be able to distinguish the latent threats in any information provided
- Ensure that all staff are briefed on the dangers of competitive intelligence and are fully aware of:
  - Who they can disclose information to
  - What information they can disclose
- Ensure that staff are sufficiently well-informed to recognise contacts from external sources which may be designed to collect intelligence
- Brief staff on the types of contacts which are likely to be suspicious
- Brief staff on the situations in which they are most likely to receive calls soliciting competitive intelligence
- Ensure that staff know that they need to report suspected competitive intelligence contacts
- Establish a reporting system to which all staff have access and through which they can communicate their findings and suspicions. This can be based on e-mail or via a dedicated software system
- Record and analyse competitive intelligence contacts
- Produce regular reports which identify:
  - The intensity of competitive intelligence calls
  - The probable originators of the calls
  - The types of information being sought
- Analyse the findings to identify the probable implications of the intelligence activity
- Define whether those suspected of collecting intelligence have the capability to use it and, if successful, the impact it could have on the business
- Assess the need for deception programmes and their practicality

Identifying the Potential Sources of Threat

The effectiveness of counter-intelligence programmes is enhanced considerably if the probable sources of attacks can be anticipated in advance. It is not too difficult to identify the main companies that could be seeking intelligence. They are likely to be known competitors, companies that have revealed an interest in entering the business and companies who, by nature of their skill base, their past history and their needs, ought to be considering entering the business. The difficulty arises with companies that have no current links with the business but may nevertheless see it as a diversification opportunity. In these cases the counter-intelligence process must itself identify the sources of threat.

An obvious first step to determine how serious companies are about studying their competitors is to check whether they have appointed staff with a responsibility for competitive intelligence. Sometimes this can be as simple as examining the annual directory of the Society of Competitive Intelligence Professionals, which lists members. More commonly, those practising the art within companies do not like to advertise their presence by joining a society, in which case calls to competitors could be used to establish whether the function, or a near relative such as business intelligence, exists. If a functional responsibility is located it is reasonable to assume that they are monitoring all of their competitors. However, the absence of an internal function does not necessarily mean that they are uninterested in their competitors. Competitive intelligence may be the part-time responsibility of a member of the marketing or market research team or they could be using external consultants.

Detecting whether a competitor is using consultants is extremely difficult. No competitive intelligence consultant publishes a list of clients and they use a variety of techniques to conceal their intent and the identity of those that have hired them. Whilst it is possible to limit the amount of intelligence the specialists can gather it is rarely possible to do better than guess who their clients are.

The identification of potential threats will rely heavily on information gathered by marketing and sales teams who are in the front line of contacts with the market, but should also involve strategic and business planning teams that are considering the future evolution of the business.

Sales and marketing teams need to briefed to provide a regular flow of information on current and potential competitors active in the market and any indications that they are actively studying their competition. The key points in the briefing will overlap with those set out for engaging sales teams in collecting competitive intelligence, namely:

- Identify the competitors most frequently encountered in the market and report continuously on their current activities
- Maintain a constant watch for information (rumours, gossip and evidence of intensifying (or diminishing) activity) indicating that current competitors are becoming more (or less) interested in the business
- Identify competitors that have a presence in the market but a low market share
- Seek information that suggests whether they will become more active in the business or whether they are likely to exit the market
- Collect and report any information that suggests that companies not active in the business are considering market entry. The most likely candidates are:
  - Companies servicing the same client base who have the technical capability to enter the market
  - Companies with technology that is capable of meeting customer needs but not currently used in the market
- Monitor market trends in order to determine whether fundamental changes are taking place in demand that would open up the market to new competitors
- Monitor supply technologies in order to determine whether new suppliers have acquired the means of entering the business

As previously noted, sales and marketing teams are a difficult resource to use in the collection of competitive intelligence. They are equally difficult to use in counter-intelligence. This is partly because sales representatives' natural paranoia may cause them to identify threats that are far from realistic and partly because it is difficult to encourage them to share information that they might be able to use for personal advantage. As with competitive intelligence, the answer is to draw them into the company's intelligence community and to permit them to help define competitive intelligence objectives and use the results of competitive analysis. Their engagement in counter-intelligence will flow naturally from the same process.

Identifying the Means By Which Intelligence is Being Sought

The word intelligence is usually associated with 'agents' or, in a more covert world, 'spies'. Whilst some of those practising competitive intelligence might like to think of themselves as James Bond, most competitive intelligence is gathered by individuals with far more modest ambitions and even more mundane titles. Indeed the more innocuous and innocent they seem the less likely they are to be detected.

Intelligence that is collected entirely from secondary sources is impossible to detect. The only defence is to assume that everything that is published by and about the company will fall into the hands of the competition and its content modulated accordingly.

Primary intelligence collection, that is, that obtained directly from sources within the company, is a different matter. All primary intelligence activities leave a trace of one kind or another, largely in the form of the identity of the individual making the enquiries. If not James Bond, who should be looked for? The list of titles that are used for competitive intelligence-gathering fall into two categories: those that are close enough to the truth to be regarded as a legitimate description of the caller and those that are a misrepresentation of the caller's true identity:

(a) Actual or near representation

- Market researchers
- Business consultants
- Management consultants
- Staff of the competitors themselves

(b) Misrepresentation

- Students (carrying out research for a thesis)
- Head-hunters
- Recruitment specialists
- Actual or potential customers
- Journalists

The first group includes those who present themselves legitimately but who fail to disclose the full purpose of their enquiries. The code of ethics under which legitimate competitive intelligence professionals collect data states that they must not misrepresent themselves. It does not state that they must explain precisely why the enquiries are being made and on whose behalf. Obviously they cannot make calls disclosing that they are employed by a competitive intelligence agency seeking information for a competitor, since this would reduce their chances of gathering anything useful to zero. On the other hand a statement to the effect that they are market researchers or business consultants seeking information for a report on a market and the activities on the businesses operating within it is close enough to the truth to satisfy most consciences.

Misrepresentation is harder to deal with and is most likely to be practised by private detective agencies, corporate investigators and individual consultants who, although they will rarely undertake tasks which are illegal, do not subscribe to the code of conduct which constrains the activities of competitive intelligence professionals. These individuals may go to considerable lengths to support their deception. This includes establishing dummy companies, allocating dedicated telephone lines to receive return calls, placing false job advertisements or having articles published in the media. They are also not averse to paying for information.

Most staff will have considerable difficulty in distinguishing genuine enquiries from those whose purpose is the collection of intelligence. A common response is to ban all discussions with third parties unless their bona fides are proven or senior management approval is given. Although secure, this approach risks alienating potential customers and frustrating a number of business activities from which most companies benefit from time to time. Conducting market research surveys is becoming increasingly difficult as companies instruct staff not to speak to outsiders under any circumstances. However, it is equally important for both customers and suppliers that the needs of the former are fully understood by the latter and frustrating the process by which this information is collected systematically and cost-effectively is to nobody's advantage. A further reason for avoiding outright bans is that, if dealt with correctly, counter-intelligence activities can themselves provide valuable competitive intelligence.

The middle path is to train staff to recognise potentially suspicious calls and to funnel them to a central department capable of probing the reasons for calls, deciding which are genuine and controlling the outflow in information.

The most obvious tell-tale signs that an intelligence exercise is under way are:

• Calls to staff from previously unknown sources and with motives that seem vague or unbelievable and who are unusually persistent

- An overdose of visitors to the company's exhibition stands
- An increase in the number of contacts with the sales force by the sales representatives of rival companies
- Requests for information from organisations that claim to be acting for an unnamed client
- Requests from students, journalists and unknown consultants
- Invitations to share information with the staff of competitors
- Enquiries from potential customers which contain requests for detailed or unusual information
- An increase in calls from head-hunters (not easy to spot since staff rarely report approaches by head-hunters)
- An upturn in market research activity within the customer base
- Initiation of contacts by staff in competitive organisations or an upturn in contacts from rival company staff who are already in touch
- Requests from anyone who refuses to leave a return telephone number

The main difficulty arises from the fact that much of this activity will pass unnoticed unless it is so blatant that it cannot fail to be commented on or the company is geared up to detect suspicious activity.

Identifying and Assessing the Vulnerabilities

A major task for the counter-intelligence unit is to assess the areas of vulnerability in the company. The task can be exceptionally difficult because the number of areas of weakness can be huge. The key vulnerabilities in all organisations lie in:

- All information issued by the company and about the company
- Corporate databases and knowledge management systems
- People
- Physical surveillance
- Accidental loss of documents and data
- Deductions

Published information and official filings

The first task in any search for information on companies is to examine all published sources. Intelligence experts scour a wide range of sources for descriptions of companies' activities and the tiniest clues to strategy. Even the most innocuous statements and the smallest items of information may add pieces to a jigsaw puzzle, which over time builds up to an increasingly precise portrait of an organisation. The most advanced may apply techniques such as semiology to advertisements in order to detect how competitors perceive themselves. The sources that can be searched include all those listed in Chapters 6 and 7.

Many of the secondary sources are essential, their content dictated by legislation, official reporting requirements or the need to communicate effectively with customers, shareholders and business partners. However, much of the information that is disseminated does not play an essential role in the business process and has more to do with corporate and individual pride or an over-inflated view of the need for openness.

The Internet has expanded the availability of information available about companies exponentially and the companies themselves originate a high proportion of what is available. Some corporate web designers, liberated from restraints imposed by cost and space, appear to have gone mad and include a variety of documentation on their sites which exposes the company to inspection by outsiders on a scale not previously practical.

The more traditional ways of disseminating information pose no less of a risk, even though they may less accessible. The materials disseminated at exhibitions and trade shows, on training courses and in open seminars can be valuable source documents, as can the content of papers presented by staff at conferences and professional meetings. There is also great value to be derived from brochures and catalogues distributed as part of the sales process. The transfer of much of this material to the Internet serves only to exacerbate the problem.

Corporate databases and knowledge management systems

In the past companies have been to some extent protected by the fact that information was fragmented throughout the organisation. Very few staff had access to anything approaching a complete database of information. Corporate databases and knowledge management systems are changing this situation by creating a central record that is accessible by large numbers of staff. Although this enhances their ability to perform their jobs it also increases the risk that data will be accessed and passed on to third parties.

People

After the published sources, the softest targets in an intelligence-gathering exercise are people. A common factor in business all over the world is that people like to talk about themselves, their work and the company that employs them. Some of the worst offenders are executives who forget the need for security when confronted with a microphone or a journalist's notebook. Others do it at all forms of social and business gatherings, with friends, with other passengers on airlines or trains, at conferences, at exhibitions, at the hairdresser – indeed in any situation where the alternative is standing or sitting silently in groups. Controlling the volume and quality of information passed out about an organisation by word of mouth is the most difficult challenge in counter-intelligence.

Staff

In all companies the main threat arises from the staff. A combination of personal characteristics – including unawareness, pride, arrogance, stupidity, envy and anger – can induce them to reveal information that is commercially sensitive. The staff that are most exposed to competitive intelligence activities are those whose role includes contact with outsiders, principally:

- Telephonists
- Receptionists
- Call centres
- Sales and marketing
- Maintenance
- Installation
- Warehouse staff
- Delivery staff
- Customer service staff
- PR/Corporate Affairs

Other staff can also be exposed but since external contact is the exception rather than the rule, they should be more alert when questioned – though it would be most unwise to rely on this observation. The very fact that they are not normally questioned by outsiders may mean that they are less aware of the dangers of revealing information.

All staff are party to the information that they need to have in order to do their jobs. This may not always be particularly sensitive but in addition to the information that they know of officially they also hear details of company activities, plans and performance on the grapevine that exists in all organisations. The difficulty with most staff lies in their inability to recognise what is sensitive and what is not. For the competitive analyst seemingly innocuous information can be extremely useful when piecing together a profile of a competitor. Telephonists who might readily recognise the inadvisability of disclosing some hearsay that the company was in financial difficulties would not necessarily see any harm in revealing the number of staff on the site, the identity of key managers or the absence or presence of specific operating departments.

Staff in the front line of contact with outsiders can be asked for information in a wide variety of situations. These include:

- Day-to-day contact with customers, potential customers, distributors and suppliers
- Direct and indirect contact with various external stakeholders and others with an interest in the company – such as investors, brokers' analysts and journalists
- Manning exhibition stands
- Participation in conferences
- Fellow passengers – particularly on aircraft

The identity of the enquirer, the situation in which the information is requested and the method of communicating (face to face, telephone conversation, e-mail or fax) all influence the willingness to respond to questions. Few would hesitate to respond to a direct question from a known customer during a sales meeting, providing it was the type of information a customer needed to have or could legitimately ask out of curiosity about a supplier. The same question from an unknown enquirer on the telephone should normally produce a negative response. However, conferences and exhibitions tend to desensitise the critical facilities to the point at which fellow delegates and stand visitors often receive responses to the most impertinent questions, despite the fact that their credentials have never been established.

Some of the most significant intelligence coups have arisen inadvertently from conversations between staff that have been overheard. Others have resulted from conversations between complete strangers who happen to be travelling together. Clearly it is a major piece of bad luck if you happen to be sitting next to a staff member from a competitor or someone working on their behalf, but the forces which bring people together are often related to the fact that they have some common interest. For example, an above-average proportion of travellers to a destination in which an industry conference is being held will have an interest in that industry. Major intelligence coups have also resulted from accidents and carelessness rather than cleverness on the part of the intelligence gatherers. Briefcases and papers left in taxis, in telephone booths, at restaurant tables and on park benches have all been gratefully received by intelligence gatherers at some stage in the past.

Ex-staff

Ex-staff can be a major area of vulnerability, particularly senior staff who have left the company under some form of cloud or nursing a grievance. Apart from high-profile cases, ex-staff are not always easy to locate. However, the chances of finding them are increasing not only because they commonly move on to companies active in the same or similar businesses but also because of the growing use of the Internet as a recruitment medium. This is resulting in a substantial number of published CVs which can be searched by previous employment record. The main protection from damage inflicted by previous employees passing on information is time. The usefulness of the information they hold in their heads or even in any documents they may have taken with them diminishes as time passes.

Not surprisingly, companies regularly debrief new recruits who have previously worked for competitors. This process can cause maximum damage since the information they have is current.

Associates and customers

The most difficult group of individuals and organisations to control are those that are outside the company but nevertheless party to information about the company's activities. These include:

- Joint venture partners
- Advisers – such as banks, lawyers, consultants, advertising agencies and PR companies
- Customers
- Suppliers
- Trade press journalists
- Stockbrokers' analysts

Some of these – most notably the professions – would be difficult information sources to attack since their profession requires them to protect the confidentiality of their clients. Others are more inclined to discuss the companies they deal with and some, such as brokers' analysts, may see a positive benefit in sharing information. When considering associates and customers it is always worth remembering that only occasionally do customers and suppliers owe any real allegiance to the companies they deal with.

Accidents

Accidents plague all organisations and some are bound to result in information finding its way to competitors. Whilst it is wrong for competitors to 'organise' accidents and it is bordering on unethical to use information that falls into their hands accidentally, the onus is on companies to protect their secrets and if they leak accidentally they cannot be too surprised if the information is used against them. The most common accidents that afflict companies are:

- Lost documents
- Lost laptop computers
- Misdirected faxes
- Overheard conversations and phone calls

Physical Surveillance

Although some forms of physical surveillance are illegal, others are not and are used regularly within the competitive intelligence process. Observing, counting, measuring and appraising can produce valuable intelligence when applied to a company's facilities, its products, those of its activities, such as transport, that can be seen externally and the staff that it employs. Although much of what a company does can be hidden from public gaze, there is even more which cannot. Company sites can be measured and what is going on within the site can be observed from the air and even by satellite. Products can be purchased and 'reverse engineered' in order to identify the technology that has been employed. Transport fleets can be counted, inward shipments of goods can be observed. The calibre of staff can be assessed at public meetings and exhibitions.

Deductions

The element of competitive intelligence that is virtually impossible to control is the use of fragmentary information as a basis for deductions about a competitor's strategy. Some elements of strategy may be publicly articulated, as in items contained in annual and quarterly reports, periodic releases to shareholders and articles written by or about the company and its senior personnel. However, even for public companies, these rarely add up to a comprehensive statement of strategy and there is usually nothing available at all for the large number of private companies. To gain insight into their competitors' strategies analysts have devised or adapted a number of tools to put together plausible additions to the incomplete data they have collected. These processes, which include brainstorming, scenarios, war gaming and a variety of computer models, can produce credible and sometimes surprisingly accurate simulations of competitors' positioning and strategy.

Categorise Information

As set out above it is not practical to protect all information within an organisation, only that which could do serious harm in the hands of a rival organisation or is assessed as being commercially sensitive. In order to mount a realistic defence it is therefore essential to classify company information according to its sensitivity. Defence measures can then be focused on the information that it is essential to protect and time and effort are not wasted on blocking competitor access to information which is not worth defending. The school of thought which says that making it difficult and therefore costly for competitors to obtain even the simplest information ignores the fact that those processes may alienate others, in particular customers, and cause loss of business. The practice of prohibiting switchboards to route calls to staff unless the caller knows the name of the person they are trying to contact may seem like a laudable and justifiable barrier – particularly as a means of preventing calls from head-hunters – but what is a genuine customer likely to do when confronted with a potential supplier that appears to be impenetrable? He usually gives up and seeks an alternative, more friendly, source of supply.

Company information can be categorised into four bands:

- Information that must remain completely confidential and defended at all cost
- Information that the company would prefer not to pass into competitors' hands but is not worth a 'spare no expense' defence
- Information which does not need to pass to third parties but is not worth defending
- Information which must pass to third parties

The criteria by which information is allocated to each category should include not only the damage that the knowledge can inflict but also the ease by which it can be obtained by other routes. Defending information incurs a cost and there is little point in paying for defence mechanisms that can be easily circumvented.

The content of each category will be specific to each company and will also vary by industry sector. However, typical categorisations will be as follows.

Highly confidential information

- Strategic and business plans
- Proprietary company technology (such as product formulations and production technology)
- R&D projects
- New product development plans
- Product launch dates
- Capacity expansion plans
- New markets being targeted
- Acquisition plans
- Planned divestments
- Segmentation strategy and target markets
- Sales by product line
- Sales by customer group
- Customer lists
- Future pricing plans
- Discount policy
- Future distribution plans
- Promotional plans (advertising, below the line and PR)

Moderately confidential information

- Staff breakdowns by division
- Staff qualifications
- Key customer accounts
- Suppliers of raw materials
- Equipment suppliers
- Production equipment installed
- Subcontractors used
- Packaging suppliers
- Volumes of packaging used
- Importance of each of the distribution channels used
- Guarantee policy

- Staff training methods
- Exhibition plans
- Future sponsorship plans
- Exports (volume and countries serviced)

Information not worth defending

- Staff numbers
- Key executives
- Ownership
- Organisational structure
- Production locations
- Patents and licences held
- Distribution channels
- Advertising media used
- Advertising expenditure
- Exhibitions attended
- Sponsorships
- Overseas subsidiaries

Information which must be provided to third parties

- Current product specifications
- Technical literature
- Impending new product launches requiring advanced publicity
- Claimed product advantages
- Product availability
- Supply points (retail and wholesale)
- Prices and discount structures
- Support services
- Maintenance services
- Guarantees offered

Reducing the Chances of Intelligence Being Obtained

It should be clear from what has been said above that it is impossible to protect all information, nor is it desirable to do so. Much of the information that flows out of any organisation is an essential part of the processes by which it does business. The requirement for counter-intelligence is to minimise the outflow of information that is commercially sensitive and to try to ensure that it does not get into the hands of the competition. The main lines of defence are to ensure:

- Close scrutiny of all written information produced by the company
- That sensitive information is, in as far as possible, confined to those that appreciate its value and can be trusted not to divulge it
- That staff and others associated with the company are well-briefed on the dangers of competitive intelligence and handle their relationships with outsiders with due care

Written information audit

All written information produced by the company must be reviewed in order to ensure that, whilst meeting the purpose for which it is required, no superfluous or highly sensitive information is contained. The audit must cover:

- Official filings which must enter the public domain (such as Annual Reports, SEC and Stock Exchange filings)
- Brochures
- Newsletters
- Recruitment advertisements
- Directory entries
- Exhibition guide entries

Everything published by the company on the Internet must be the subject of the audit as well as hard-copy documents.

Limiting the availability of information

'Need to know' is a basic rule of intelligence that ensures that staff have access only to the information they need for the roles they fill. However, it is extremely difficult to apply in a civilian organisation mainly because, between themselves, staff do not normally conform to security practices that are applied regularly in the military. Natural curiosity about the organisation they work for and a moderately active rumour mill generally ensures that information circulates through unofficial channels more quickly than it can be disseminated officially. Furthermore, the current thrust of employee relations and initiatives such as Investors in People is to encourage employers to make staff party to business plans and the strategic direction of the company that employs them. It is felt that openness, participation and consultation will encourage staff to pull together within the company, increase enthusiasm and improve productivity. Whatever the theory and its impact on performance, the result is that staff are party to more of the type of information which could damage the company if it was passed to competitors.

Press, analyst and shareholder briefings must be carefully controlled. All information passed to any of these groups immediately enters the public domain and it must be assumed that it will inevitably find its way to competitors.

Whatever the company policy, it is the day-to-day actions by staff that determine the extent to which intelligence will leak out of the organisation. Venetian glass manufacturers sought to protect their secrets by confining their staff to the island of Murano, where it was virtually impossible for them to meet outsiders and disclose information. Extreme measures like incarceration cannot be applied today and management must rely on careful staff briefings to instil the discipline that will minimise information outflows. Staff should be told to assume that everything they write or discuss with third parties could find its way to a competitor and its content should be judged accordingly. However, taken to an extreme, this approach could stifle the company's ability to do business. Customers and distributors will generally react badly if a supplier displays a tendency to paranoia. The solution is to develop a body of information that it is acceptable to release to outsiders, for whatever purpose, and to instruct staff that no information should be released beyond that contained in the documents. An increasing number of companies are enshrining this instruction in their terms of employment, thus giving them the power to discipline staff who are found to be in breach of standard operating procedures.

Documents

Documents released by the company have been identified as a major potential source of vulnerability and must be prepared and handled accordingly. Some simpler rules to follow are:

- All documents for release outside the company should be vetted to ensure that they contain the minimum information to meet the needs of the purpose for which they are designed – superfluous information increases the chances that valuable intelligence will be divulged
- All information published on open Internet sites must be treated even more carefully than published documents. Whilst there is some control over the distribution of company documents, there is absolutely no control over access to public sites on the Internet
- If the Internet is felt to be a useful method of distributing information, consider the use of closed sites with access by password only. This can give some measure of control over who sees the data

- No interviews can be given to journalists (for the national or trade press) unless the company has the right to review the content of the resulting article and to exclude from it any information that is subsequently thought to be dangerous
- Copies of all internal documents should be numbered so that in the event of a leak the source can (possibly) be traced
- Keep copies of all sensitive documents in locked cabinets
- Password-protect all computer files and strictly control access to the passwords
- Documents must not be taken off the company's premises unless for a purpose for which the document was designed

Conversations

Conversations with third parties constitute a major risk and the onus is on all staff to verify the bona fides of the individuals making requests for information, establish that the reasons for the enquiries are genuine and regulate what they say. The basic ground rules should be as follows:

- Verify the credentials of all organisations whose staff approach you for information. This should include:
  - The name of the company
  - The company's location
  - The telephone number and the extension to call back to
  - The business in which the company is active
- Verify the identity and job function of the person calling
- Ask for a clear explanation of why the information is being requested and the purpose to which it is being put
- If the information is said to be required for another organisation ask for the identity of that organisation. If the identity is not revealed, either establish the bona fides of the intermediary and that the client's use of them is genuine or refuse to provide information and suggest that the client company makes direct contact
- Test the responses given for accuracy by asking a few simple questions. For example, if the enquirer states that the information is required for a market survey ask the name of the sponsor of the survey, the aspects of the market that are to be analysed and the sources of information that are being used. (Note: a genuine market researcher will normally volunteer this information at the outset)

- If not satisfied that the reason for requesting the information is genuine, ask for written confirmation (letter, fax or e-mail) stating the information required and the purpose to which it will be put
- Check with close colleagues to see if similar calls have been received
- Report all suspicious calls to the staff member responsible for counter-intelligence, regardless of whether any response has been given reporting:

  - The timing of the call
  - The identity of the caller
  - The stated reason for the request
  - The information requested
  - The reason for suspicion
  - The action taken

Briefing sales staff

Sales staff (working in the field and in telesales centres) are a major source of vulnerability. Their primary task is rarely easy and they generally feel that they need all the help they can get. A major part of their role is to provide clients and potential clients with information that will convince them that the product or service will meet their needs and that the company is a credible supplier. In fulfilling this role there is an ever-present temptation to maximise the information they provide and step over the boundary of what is reasonable. This commonly happens when they are confronted with a customer who is proving difficult to convince and who is asking for increasingly detailed information. There is an additional risk that sales staff will be less discriminating in whom they provide information to. Thus anyone who, however vaguely, indicates that they could be a buyer may be able to access intelligence from members of the sales force.

The sales training process must include a component that provides guidance on recognising genuine prospects and on controlling the levels of information provided, even during the thrill of the chase for business. Sales briefings need to be tailored to each business sector and the company itself but should include instructions such as:

- Verify that all those who identify themselves as potential customers could legitimately be so
- Meter the flow of information in accordance with an assessment of how likely business is to result from the contract. In other words those whose interest is judged to be casual should be provided

minimal information but more information can be provided as the level of interest in buying increases

- Establish 'levels of interest milestones' which you will use as pointers for the provision of more detailed information. For example,

  - The provision of detailed information on the buying organisation
  - Detailed statements of the use to which the product will be put
  - Written specifications or requirements
  - Agreement to a personal meeting to discuss requirements
  - Making some written or financial commitment to buy

  could all be used as triggers for the release of more detailed information on the product and the supplier

Briefing of staff providing press, analyst and shareholder briefings

Those whose role is to deal with the press and, in the case of public companies, with brokers' analysts and shareholders, require additional guidelines of which the most important are:

- It is generally assumed that all publicity is good publicity; this is not true if it results in sensitive information being channelled to competitors
- All three groups can be very demanding in terms of the level of disclosure they seek
- Whilst analysts and shareholders can be assumed to have a healthy interest in the performance of the company, the sustainability of performance in the future and the factors which are contributing to performance, the desire to create a favourable impression that will result in an improvement in the share price (or the success of a floatation or a placement of shares with investors) needs to balanced against the dangers that will arise from the information passing into the hands of competitors
- The interest of the press in a company is usually less benign. Their primary concern is to sell their newspapers or magazines and in this respect detailed and sensational stories about companies are preferable to bland news items. As with the analysts, the usefulness of press coverage in reaching a wide audience of potential customers and creating a favourable impression of the company must be balanced against the harm that excessive disclosure can do

Briefing of affiliates and customers

Affiliates of all kinds are more difficult to brief than staff partly because anything that is said may threaten the relationship and partly because, in the final analysis, there is little that can be done to control what they say. Nevertheless it is worth setting out some guidelines in an attempt to control the amount of information they pass on to third parties. This could take the form of a reminder that the relationship between a supplier and its customers and affiliates has to be one of mutual trust. In order to do business together it must be possible to have a full exchange of information, including that which is confidential and commercially sensitive and which could cause damage if it got into the hands of competitors. Customers and affiliates must also supply sensitive information and it is to the advantage of all parties that confidences are protected.

Briefing staff attending exhibitions, trade shows and conferences

The exposure to staff questioning by competitors is heightened when they travel off site. Exhibitions, trade shows and conferences all provide multiple legitimate opportunities for them to be approached outside the protective cocoon of their offices and internal security systems. At exhibitions and trade shows it is often difficult to distinguish between inquirers with a legitimate purpose and those whose objectives are only to obtain intelligence. On exhibition stands it is also difficult to prevent conversations with clients or potential clients being overheard by other visitors. The congregation of staff in public areas such as restaurants, receptions and rest rooms further increases the chances of indiscreet conversations being overheard.

It is almost inevitable that in the general excitement of an event and the multiplicity of contacts that are made defences will be lowered, a process that may be exacerbated if alcohol is available. Paradoxically, the level of vulnerability is at its highest in the slack periods, lunchtimes, the times when especially interesting activities are being mounted and the wind-down period at the end of a show. At these times the flow of visitors to stands abates, senior staff leave and the stands are manned by juniors, who suddenly find themselves in the limelight and eager to prove their worth. This is when intelligence analysts know they can make a kill.

Simple precautions can reduce some of the problems, for example by ensuring that all presentations and sensitive discussions are held in private areas and not in the open where they may be overheard and by carefully examining the credentials of all visitors before they are given information. Briefing those staff that attend conferences, trade shows and exhibitions on the dangers that are present can tighten defences. This should take the form of a general briefing to staff likely to attend events and specific briefings before any event at which the company is exhibiting. The general briefing is an essential catch-all since counter-intelligence staff may not always have the opportunity to make a specific briefing.

The briefings should cover:

- The need for all of those attending conferences and exhibitions to exercise great care when engaging in discussions with anyone they meet, even if it appears to be a chance encounter
- The need for particular discretion when holding conversations with colleagues about business matters
- Possible methods of recognising intelligence gatherers
- The standard methods used by intelligence gatherers
- Methods of establishing the credentials of all questioners before information is supplied without alienating genuine customers
- The limits of what it is permissible to disclose

The briefings could usefully involve the company's own competitive intelligence staff who can impart the tricks of the trade and recount useful war stories of their successes as a warning.

Briefing staff about to leave the organisation

The leavers can only be cautioned on the inadvisability of revealing company secrets plus a warning that they and their new employer could be held liable should any serious damages arise from their disclosures. Their loyalty will inevitably be to their new employer but there are some appeals that may work over and above the threat of sanctions. For example:

- We trust that you have enjoyed your time working with the company and that the skills and information you have gained from that experience will stand you in good stead in your future career. Not all of what you have learnt from us will be of use to you, but much of what you know about us could be of high interest to our competitors. We therefore request that you be circumspect in what you say about this company either to your new employer or to third parties
- It is always inadvisable to disclose information about previous employers too readily. Your new employer may regard it as

unethical and refuse to accept or use the information you proffer and the fact that you offered it may jeopardise your career prospects
- If asked for information about us, remember that passing on trade secrets may be deemed to be theft, which is a criminal offence
- It is also worth remembering that you may have been hired only to obtain information and once you have given it you may cease to be useful

None of these points will have much effect on those who leave the company harbouring a grievance, either because they have been fired or because they feel they have been badly treated by the company. These individuals may deliberately seek to damage the company by revealing information.

Non-disclosure agreements

Management can reinforce its briefings with non-disclosure agreements. In the case of staff these can be incorporated into the terms of employment, where the sanctions that will be applied in the event of any unauthorised disclosure can be spelt out. Non-disclosure agreements can also be requested from external organisations to whom sensitive information may need to be made available, notably customers, suppliers and business partners. These will not necessarily stop information disclosure but they will make those that sign them aware of the fact that they have a duty to maintain confidentiality. The non-disclosure agreement should typically contain:

- A statement outlining why confidentiality is required
- The types of information that are covered by the agreement
- The types of organisation to which information should not be provided
- The circumstances under which a release from the agreement may be granted
- The steps that need to be taken in order to gain a release

Suppliers and business partners will tend to take such agreements more seriously than customers, mainly because they stand to lose business if they are found breaking the agreement. Supplier and partner agreements can therefore be worded strongly, spelling out the sanctions that can result from breaches in confidentiality. Customers need to be handled more carefully, since they can always take their business elsewhere, but there is no harm in reminding them of their obligation.

Testing the System

Once a counter-intelligence system has been established its effectiveness should be tested regularly. This can be done quite effectively, by commissioning a competitive intelligence exercise on the company itself. The exercise needs to be carried out by an intelligence organisation that has no prior knowledge of the company and the effectiveness of the defence system should be judged by:

- The amount of intelligence that is gathered
- The accuracy of the intelligence
- The ease with which the intelligence is collected

Any such test is of course a test of the effectiveness of the intelligence-gathering organisation as well as of the defence system and a wholly negative result should be treated with caution.

Monitoring the Threat

Competitive intelligence programmes are rarely one-offs. They are normally mounted at regular intervals either by the same or different competitors. The threat is continuous. This means that there can be no let-up in the counter-intelligence programme. Management and staff must be continuously vigilant, recognising when programmes are being directed against them and attempting to identify the sources of attack. The attacks are likely to occur in waves initiated by any event that disturbs the equilibrium in the competitive environment, such as:

- The launch of a new product
- The introduction of a new production technology (even if thought to be a closely guarded secret)
- Bids for a major contract
- Changes in the direction or intensity of marketing activities
- The emergence of a new competitor in the business

The three key problems in spotting an 'intelligence attack' are:

- Bringing together the data in a way in which changes in the level of activity can be detected
- Covering attempted contacts with an entire company, especially in the case of large multi-site organisations
- Covering contacts with related third parties such as customers, suppliers, partners and advisers

To overcome these problems some companies have installed call-monitoring systems on which a central record of incoming 'suspicious' calls can be logged and made accessible to all staff. These systems provide staff with the facility to check how many calls have been received previously from:

- The same person
- The same organisation
- The same telephone number

The systems can also log the nature of the enquiry made during each call. A high frequency of calls from a specific source can signal an attack but a more significant warning is given when:

- The same individual calls from different numbers
- The same telephone number appears for different company names
- Different staff call from the same company

Publicise Willingness to Take Legal Action

The failure of the public at large to recognise the real difference between competitive intelligence and industrial espionage provides an opportunity to stifle the more overt activities by publicising any attacks that are detected. Recent high-profile cases (of industrial espionage), such as Oracle's attempt to obtain intelligence which proved that Microsoft was funding an apparently independent lobby group to influence the antitrust case against Microsoft, have ended up with the press criticising Oracle heavily. This resulted from their use of a detective agency that chose to obtain the information by attempting to buy the lobby group's rubbish.

The risk of embarrassing disclosures will not stop attempts to gain intelligence but may serve to curb the intensity of the approaches that are used.

Implementation

The implementation of each of the steps defined above requires one or more of the following:

- Investment in people and time
- Investment in systems and software
- Staff briefings
- Changes to employment contracts

The resources required for counter-intelligence are primarily people and time. In large and small organisations the resources may be the same as those devoted to the collection of competitive intelligence. A close alliance between the two tasks ensures that the information spin-off from counter-intelligence is fully exploited in the competitive intelligence programmes. The scale of the need for dedicated counter-intelligence personnel is driven by:

- The size of the organisation, and therefore the scale of the counter-intelligence task
- The volume and sensitivity of the information to be protected
- The amount of damage that can be inflicted by competitors

Large, multi-site organisations with substantial volumes of highly sensitive information to protect and whose performance could be very vulnerable to an informed competitive attack should certainly consider a dedicated counter-intelligence manager. In smaller organisations with lower levels of vulnerability counter-intelligence could be a part-time function.

If a security team is employed there is obviously some overlap between their tasks and counter-intelligence, though they have a much closer relationship with counter-espionage. Security teams are primarily concerned with the prevention of trespass, theft, vandalism and sabotage largely by preventing unauthorised physical intrusion into the company's sites. Maintaining physical security requires a totally different skill set to that required for counter-intelligence and there is little real point in trying to combine the two activities.

Investment systems and software are an additional resource that can be considered only when the scale of the task is sufficiently large and complex to justify the sums involved. The main systems that exist at present monitor incoming telephone calls and analyse them as identified above.

Systems permit any staff member receiving an enquiry from an external source to check, before responding:

- Whether the caller, the company from which they have stated they are calling from and the telephone number from which the call is being made have been encountered before
- The staff members they have spoken to
- The enquiries they have made

Such systems provide a powerful defence against repeated telephoning, which is one of the standard research tools used in competitive intelligence.

Staff and business partner briefings are required to alert staff and business partners to the dangers of competitive intelligence, the means by which they can detect that they are being targeted for intelligence and the actions they should take in the event that they suspect that they are being targeted.

Changes to contracts can be used to support the staff briefings by giving contractual weight to the need to protect proprietary information. The contracts that need to be considered are:

- Employment contracts issued to staff
- Contracts issued to suppliers of raw materials, equipment and services
- Contracts with joint venture partners
- If appropriate, contracts with customers and clients

It is not necessary to draw up contracts specifically to cover the need to protect proprietary information, only to add clauses to existing contracts. These should prohibit the disclosure of all company information to third parties, unless it is essential for the performance of the task being carried out for the company. The weakest links in the chain are customers and they obviously need to be handled carefully. Staff, suppliers and joint venture partners are dependent on the company for income and stand to lose if they are found in breach of contract. Customers are not beholden to the company in the same way, though they are not immune to sanctions if they reveal information that is damaging to their suppliers.

Note

1. 'Corporate Spying Firms Thrive', *The Wall Street Journal Europe*, 4 July 2000.

19 Deception and Misinformation

A major task both of (national) intelligence and security authorities is to hamper the intelligence gathering of unfriendly powers. This is done not only by restricting their intelligence gathering activities, but also by inducing them to draw incorrect conclusions from such information they do acquire ... Although it is not possible to prevent the enemy from acquiring some information, it is possible to ensure that the intelligence he does so acquire is misleading or false.[1]

The use of deception and misinformation programmes by companies seems highly attractive but must be treated with care and to be successful three conditions must be fulfilled.

- The company carrying out the deception programme must have reasonable insight into the intelligence and opinions that competitors hold on them
- The company must have a sufficiently secure system to ensure reasonable control of the information flowing out of the company
- There must be channels of communication between the deceiver and the competitors that the deceiver can control

Deception offers an opportunity to achieve the element of surprise that is so valuable in competitive marketing.

Deception and misinformation cover all types of information that can be deliberately 'spun' into the marketplace or passed directly to competitors. It also includes procedures that shield activities from competitor observation. The process is dangerous, primarily because:

- Competitors are not the only organisations that could be deceived and harm could be done to customer, supplier and partner relationships
- Maintaining a consistently deceptive story from all parts of the organisation requires an effort which may be out of all proportion to the impact it will achieve

Despite the fact that it is fraught with problems, deception is nevertheless worth considering since, if it works, it represents a major competitive action in its own right. Warfare abounds with examples of deception campaigns that were designed to 'mislead the enemy into doing something, or not doing something, so that his strategic or tactical position would be weakened'.[2] These range from the Trojan Horse to the elaborate campaigns designed to conceal the fact that the invasion of France in 1944 would commence in Normandy and the deceptive information that is planted in documents on order to trap plagiarists and illicit users. In a recent case, the United Kingdom Ordnance Survey, which sells its database of maps of the country to other map publishers as well as direct to users, proved that the AA had made illicit use of its database by planting false information. These included extra stream tributaries, imaginary farm buildings, tiny kinks in rivers, exaggerated curves in roads and missing apostrophes in names.[3]

It is tempting to think that comparable commercial activities could be used to put competitors off their guard or persuade them to waste resources responding to activities that will never take place.

Intelligence Held on the Company

The first requirement is to assess the intensity with which competitors study their competition and the methods that they use. This is a routine competitive intelligence topic that will show whether the competitors will be receptive to a deception programme. Competitors that are not in any way curious about the competitive environment in which they are operating will be difficult to deceive. Those that actively and continuously seek competitive intelligence will provide multiple deception opportunities, though they may also be more adept at distinguishing truth from fiction.

In order to provide a platform for a deception programme the company needs to determine what competitors know about them. In the first instance this is a process that can be allied with the requirement to test the intelligence defences described in the previous chapter. An inward-looking competitive intelligence programme will provide a good indication of the intelligence competitors are able to collect and, if analysed according to the first principle of competitive intelligence, will indicate the deductions that competitors have drawn. To be most effective this exercise should be carried out by an independent agency briefed to provide the most insightful report possible within the levels of budget competitors would be likely to deploy.

The main weaknesses in the analysis is that it will be difficult to build in the intelligence that competitors have access to from their internal sources such as the sales force or from previous employees. Nor is it easy to replicate the interpretation of the intelligence that has gone on within competitors. This could however be corrected by an intelligence-gathering activity designed to uncover the perceptions of the company that each of its competitors holds. This approach is used as a method of seeking additional intelligence within a normal competitive intelligence programme but comes into its own when planning a deception campaign.

Channels of Communication

The feasibility of launching a deception programme is enhanced if the company has access to communication channels that can be relied on to pass intelligence to competitors. External sources that would be perceived as being independent are preferable to company sources even though they are difficult to identify and control. Whoever is considered would have to have a close relationship with the company and would have to be party to the deception. The dangers this poses can be so great that in many instances it should be discounted.

Internal Sources of Information

A misinformation campaign is practical only if there is a nominated source in the company for all information requested by unknown third parties to whom all enquirers are automatically referred. Many companies already direct enquirers to the Public Affairs or PR officer as the sole source of information. When this is done it is possible to exert some control over the information that is released and avoid the risk that different staff will 'sing from different hymn sheets'. An authoritative Public Affairs officer is in a strong position to misinform since callers' natural tendency will be to believe, rather than challenge, what they are told, especially if they can be convinced that they have coaxed a nugget of intelligence from an unwilling respondent.

To further aid the believability of the data given out the nominated source can co-opt other staff members to assist in deceptions on a case-by-case basis. One of the tests of the accuracy of intelligence is the identity of the sources from which it has been acquired. The two key questions are:

- Is the respondent likely to know the information?
- Can the respondent be believed?

Whereas legitimate competitive intelligence gatherers are bound by a code of ethics not to deceive, no such constraints exist on those giving information. It is therefore possible to set up either a genuine source with the right credentials or a spurious information source with a convincing title whose role is to provide misleading information which either confirms the information given by the initial source or elaborates on it.

In order to avoid confusing those who have a legitimate interest in the company, misinformation should be leaked in such a way that it reaches only the ears of those for whom it is intended. Generally this means that it must be told directly to sources rather than disseminated though press releases or interviews with journalists. However, it should be borne in mind that normal information channels, particularly the press, will often contain inaccurate information. The misinformation process may dictate that no attempt is made to correct such errors, providing they are unlikely to harm the company's business.

Types of Deception

Deception can cover:

- Information collected from the company
- Observations of the company's activities
- Information disseminated about other competitors

Deception by information

To work, information passed out in deception campaigns has to be believed. This means that it must be reasonably, though not necessarily entirely, consistent with what is generally known about the company. Competitive intelligence analysts are used to the need to reconcile conflicting information. This is a natural consequence of the way in which intelligence is gathered from a variety of sources, some of whom are well-informed and some of whom are relatively uninformed. Deliberately adding misinformation to the data available for analysis makes it less likely that the outcome will be accurate. However, this is a rather crude outcome from the deception process. A more sophisticated approach would be to deceive competitors in such a way that they reach a predetermined erroneous conclusion and change their own actions accordingly. This is relatively easy with facts and internal opinions or assessments such as:

- New product developments – type and timing
- Launch dates for new products, which can be extended or reduced to confuse competitors
- Geographical expansion programmes
- Staff numbers
- Organisational structures
- Production capacities
- The relative importance of distribution channels
- Strengths and capabilities
- Weaknesses and vulnerabilities

It is much more difficult with topics that can be independently verified or checked for consistency with information publicly available about the company.

The requirement for credibility means that the misinformation must stand a chance of passing normal sanity checks. Figures that are totally inconsistent with industry norms and the experience of other suppliers will be quickly discarded as erroneous. It is therefore sensible to 'bend' the truth rather than to distort it completely. Thus, embellishments, stretching the facts or exaggerations are preferable to complete lies, providing they achieve the desired effect. There is little point in releasing information which exaggerates your staff numbers by only 10 per cent; since they will always assume a margin of error in the data, this level of distortion will do little to change the competitors' perception of your capabilities. It would be more worthwhile to concentrate on misleading competitors about the skills that are present or lacking in the workforce.

Deception by observation

Physical deception – disguising or concealing what is going on – has been widely used to provide an enemy with false observations. It is a staple activity in wartime and is still used regularly by the automobile industry when road-testing new models for which the styling and performance features need to be kept confidential until the models are launched. Unfortunately, the motor industry's practice is well-known, as are the normal test locations, and motoring journals spend considerable sums on advance pictures and artistic representations of new models. But this does not invalidate the use of physical deception in other areas.

The types of deceptions that could work in the competitive arena include:

- Camouflage – a wartime favourite for concealing what exists in the way of military hardware either by covering items or by changing their shape. In civilian operations, camouflage can be used to distort the intelligence gained by aerial or satellite reconnaissance of company sites
- Dummy activities – the competitive equivalent of dummy tanks and aircraft used to deceive the enemy into raising their estimates of resources could be the 'deliberate loss' of documents describing company resources and plans in a way or place which would be likely to result in them finding their way to a competitor
- False campaigns – test-marketing programmes are used regularly to determine how a new product will perform and are watched eagerly by competitors. A false test-marketing programme using a different product and/or a different marketing approach would be an expensive but highly effective method of deceiving the competition

Physical deception requires innovative thought and a sense of theatre to be successful. It may also be such fun that the budget it demands is out of proportion to the effect it achieves. When it is vitally important that the competition is deceived, a significant deception campaign may be justified but if this is not the case the activity should be treated with considerable caution.

Ethical Considerations

Deception involves telling lies and it may be challenged whether this is ethically acceptable. Whilst telling lies about competitors' activities in order to harm their business is unethical, it can be argued that lying in order to protect one's own business interests is ethical. Indeed it could be said that although there is always an option to say nothing, in some circumstances it could be unethical to tell the truth if by doing so the interests of the owners and employees could be damaged.

Propaganda

Deception does not necessarily stop at the company itself. Consider-able mileage may be gained by disseminating false information about competitors, the equivalent of the 'black art' of propaganda used in wartime. As with all false information, care must be taken to ensure that it is credible and is not libellous, but there is little doubt that carefully placed rumours will be readily absorbed by the marketplace and can cause havoc to competitors' plans and force them onto the defensive. These activities can be used to buy time or act as a smokescreen for developments.

The main problem facing the propagandist is that the activities may trigger retaliatory action. False information is easy to place and all companies can engage in the process if they so wish. An escalating propaganda war could do considerable harm to all participants in a market. A secondary problem arises if the propagandist is found out. Such a discovery would inevitably lead to considerable opprobrium being heaped on the head of the propagandist and a loss of reputation on a scale that could damage business.

There is no doubt that misinformation, deception and propaganda can be very useful weapons in the competitive battle not only as defence mechanisms but also as a means of attack. They are, however, fraught with dangers and are not for the faint-hearted. If there is any doubt that they will be successful they are probably better avoided. As far as is known they are not widely practised even though it is a logical activity to undertake. Time spent thinking about deception could pay off but might be more valuable as a source of entertainment than a contribution to strategic advantage.

Notes

1. Michael Howard, *British Intelligence in the Second World War* (London, Her Majesty's Stationery Office, 1989).
2. Charles Cruickshank, *Deception in World War II* (Oxford, Oxford University Press, 1979).
3. *The Times*, 6 March 2001.

Appendix: The Competitive Intelligence Checklist

The coverage of any competitive intelligence exercise will vary according to business area, the companies to be covered and the purposes for which the results will be used. The checklist that follows lists the generic topics that can be covered.

(A) Who Are the Competitors?

- Current direct competitors
- Current indirect competitors
- Potential future competitors

(B) Profiles of Current and Potential Competitors

1. Company details

- Headquarters
- Company structure
- Production locations
- Sales offices (domestic and foreign)
- Key executives (background, previous employment, track record)
- Total number of employees (administration, production and sales and marketing)
- Ownership
- Subsidiaries
- Affiliates

2. Organisation

- Organisational structure
- Key operating divisions
- Resourcing of each division
- Activities of each division

3. Financial performance

- Consolidated key financial performance data
- Divisional financial performance

4. Products

- Products/services supplied
- Specifications of products/services
- Claimed technical/specification advantages
- Major product applications
- New product development
- Investment in R&D (history)

5. Production

- Production employees
- Production capacity
- Capacity expansion plans
- Production technologies
- Claimed production skills
- Licences held/given

6. Suppliers

- Raw material suppliers
- Equipment suppliers
- Subcontractors used
- Packaging suppliers
- Length of time suppliers have been used
- Use of electronic data exchange
- E-procurement (see section on e-business)

7. Sales and customer base

- Size and structure of the sales force
- Characteristics of the sales force (technical or commercial)
- Qualifications of the sales staff
- Length of time sales representatives have been with the company
- Role of the sales staff (representation, order-taking, provision of technical advice)
- Use of field sales agencies
- Total sales (volume and value)

- Key accounts/customers and contribution to total business
- Contribution of each product/service line to company sales
- Sales by applications
- Sales growth

8. After-sales and technical support

- Types of support provided
- Support methods (telephone, on-site, return of items to support centre, Internet)
- Number of support staff
- Number of maintenance personnel
- Qualifications of the support and maintenance staff
- Regional organisation
- Use of technical literature, CD-Roms, video and other methods of distributing technical information

9. Physical distribution

- Distribution channels used
- Key distributors
- Relative importance of each distribution channel
- Distribution methods (own transport resources, subcontracted logistics services)
- Size and structure of transport fleet
- Use of vehicle livery for advertising

10. Marketing

- Target market segments
- Market shares in key segments
- Size and structure of the sales and marketing department
- Outline of marketing and promotion methods
- Brochures and catalogues
  - Format
  - Coverage
  - Content
- Newsletters
- Advertising
  - Advertising objectives
  - Advertising expenditure

– Media used (TV, radio, national press, trade, technical and professional press, cinema, posters and non-conventional media)
– Advertising messages
– Advertising agencies used
- Direct marketing
  – Direct mail programmes
  – Telesales
  – Role of the telesales department
  – Balance between inbound and outbound activity
  – Locations of call centres
  – Number of telesales agents
  – Sources of databases
- PR (programmes and resources)
  – Agencies used
  – News items issued
  – Volume of coverage obtained
- Sales promotion
  – Programmes
  – Incentives
  – Resources
- Exhibitions attended
- Sponsorship
  – Events sponsored
  – Value of sponsorships
- Corporate hospitality
  – Events used
- Merchandising
- Customer/distributor service programmes
- Market research
  – Commitment to research
  – Size of research department
  – Types of research carried out

11. Website

- Role of the website within the e-business strategy (see below)
- Format (text, graphics)
- Coverage and content
- Extent to which the website is transactional and types of transactions available
- Hyperlinks to other sites
- Number of visitors/hits to website

12. E-business

- Existence of an e-business strategy
- Role of e-business in the overall strategy
- E-business objectives
- E-business initiatives
  - Electronic information exchanges with suppliers and customers
  - E-procurement
  - Transactional services (ordering, inventory data, order status, payment information, payments)
- Proportion of sales made through e-business channels
- Use of Internet trading sites
- Use of extranets and web portals

13. Prices and discounts

- Price of ranges per product line
- Price positioning
- Discount structure

14. Relationships/partnerships

- Licences
- Joint ventures
- Distribution agreements
- Marketing partnerships
- Length of time relationships/partnerships have been running
- Affiliations/membership of trade bodies

15. Export activity

- Export sales
- Importance of exports in total revenues
- Export methods (through overseas subsidiaries, agents, distributors)
- Countries in which export sales are made and local resources in each country
- Export marketing activity

16. Overseas subsidiaries

- Countries
- Locations
- Activities (representation, local production, sales and marketing)
- Products sold
- Contribution to consolidated revenues

(C) Interpretation

The data collected on each company can be analysed and interpreted in order to deduce those aspects of their activities on which direct information is unlikely to collected. These will include:

- Apparent overall strategic intent
- Strategic directions
- Methods of implementing the strategy
  - Apparent market positioning
  - Products
  - Technology
  - Target markets (customer segments, geographical)
  - Apparent distribution strategy
  - Apparent pricing strategy
  - Promotion and communications strategy
- Extent and nature of competitive threat
- Resources and resource limitations on the business
- Potential retaliation to competitive action (intensity and direction)

(D) Counter-Intelligence

On the assumption that all companies seeking competitive intelligence are also likely to be the subject of competitive intelligence-gathering exercises by their competitors, equal consideration should be given to the task of minimising information outflows. A key task is to balance essential information outflows (for marketing, procurement and other purposes) with the need to restrict information flows to competitors or those acting on their behalf. The relevant questions to be asked are:

- Who is likely to be seeking information about our activities?
- What information needs to be protected?
- Who has access to the information?
  - Within the organisation
  - Externally
- Are we vulnerable to information outflows from distributors?
- Are we vulnerable to information outflows from customers?
- Are we vulnerable to information outflows from advisers and consultants?
- Have those with access to the information signed confidentiality agreements?

- What physical measures are in place to prevent/control information outflows?
  - From full-time employed staff
  - From part-time staff
  - From the staff of distributors and associates
  - By observation
- Who screens all documents passing out of the company for their information content?
  - Brochures and catalogues
  - Newsletters
  - Annual reports
  - Other official filings

Further Reading

Competition

R. D'Aveni, *Hyper-Competition*, The Free Press, New York, 1994.

L. Fahey, *Competitors*, John Wiley, New York, 1999.

J. Moore, *The Death of Competition*, HarperBusiness, New York, 1996.

M. Porter, *Competitive Strategy*, The Free Press, New York, 1980.

M. Porter, *Competitive Advantage*, Macmillan, New York, 1985.

M. Porter, *The Competitive Advantage of Nations*, The Free Press, New York, 1990.

M. Porter, *On Competition*, Harvard Business School Press, Boston, 2000.

D. Ramsey, *The Corporate Warriors*, Houghton Mifflin Company, Boston, 1987.

C. Stern and G. Stalk Jr (eds), *Perspectives on Strategy*, John Wiley, New York, 1998.

M. Treacy and F. Wiersema, *The Discipline of Market Leaders*, Addison-Wesley, Reading MA, 1996.

Marketing Warfare

C. von Clausewitz, *On War*, Penguin Classics, Harmondsworth, 1983.

R. Duro and B. Sandstrom, *The Basic Principles of Marketing Warfare*, John Wiley, Chichester, Sussex, 1987.

A. Ries and J. Trout, *Marketing Warfare*, McGraw-Hill, New York, 1986.

Sun Tzu (ed. J. Clavell), *The Art of War*, Delacorte Press, New York, 1983.

Competitive Intelligence

H.P. Burwell, *Online Competitive Intelligence*, Facts on Demand Press, Tempe AZ, 1999.

L. Fuld, *The New Competitive Intelligence*, John Wiley, New York, 1995.

D. Hussey and P. Jenster, *Competitor Intelligence*, John Wiley, Chichester, 1999.

L. Kanahar, *Competitive Intelligence*, Simon & Schuster, New York, 1996.

R. Linville, *CI Boot Camp*, Society of Competitive Intelligence Professionals, Alexandria VA, 1996.

J. McGonagle and C. Vella, *A New Archetype for Competitive Intelligence*, Quorum Books, Westport, 1996.

J. Nolan, *Confidential*, HarperBusiness, New York, 1999.

A. Pollard, *Competitive Intelligence*, Financial Times Pitman Publishing, London, 1999.
K. Tyson, *The Complete Guide to Competitive Intelligence*, K. Tyson International, Chicago, 1998.
How to Find Business Intelligence in Washington, Washington Researchers, 1997.
How to Find Information on Private Companies, Washington Researchers, 1999.

Industrial Espionage

H. Cornwall, *The Industrial Espionage Handbook*, Century, 1991.
P. Hamilton, *Espionage and Subversion in an Industrial Society*, Hutchinson, London, 1967.
I. Winkler, *Corporate Espionage*, Prima Publishing, Rocklin CA, 1997.

Techniques Useful to Competitive Analysts

D. Bernstein, *Put Together, Put It Across*, Cassell, London, 1988.
B. Cooper, *Writing Technical Reports*, Penguin, London, 1964.
E. Gowes, *The Complete Plain Words*, HMSO, London, 1954.
R. Hoff, *'I Can See You Naked': A Fearless Guide to Making Presentations*, Andrew and McMeel, Kansas City MS, 1988.
J. Honeycutt, *Using the Internet* (3rd edn), Que, Indianapolis IN, 1997.
R. Jolles, *How to Run Seminars and Workshops*, John Wiley, New York, 1993.
M. Moroney, *Facts from Figures*, Penguin, London, 1992.
J. Paterson, *Sign Here*, Ashgrove Press, Bath, 1998.
E. Tufte, *The Visual Display of Quantative Information*, Graphics Press, Cheshire, Conneticut, 1983.
K. Waterhouse, *English our English*, Viking Books, London, 1992.

Knowledge Management

V. Allee, *The Knowledge Evolution – Expanding Organisational Intelligence*, Butterworth-Heinemann, London, 1997.
T. Davenport and L. Prusak, *Working Knowledge: How Organisations Manage What They Know*, Harvard Business School Press, Boston, 1997.
R. Ruggles (ed.), *Knowledge Management Tools – Resources for the Knowledge Based Economy*, Butterworth-Heinemann, London, 1997.

Index